CONTENTS   مُحْتَوَيات أَلْكِتاب

Spoken Arabic for English Speakers

Part One

Introduction أَلْمُقِدِمَة	III
Important Learning Notes	1
Lesson 1: this is + an object	3
Directions to be followed rigorously	7
Lesson 2: Bring something please.	8
The prefixes "the" & "and" in Arabic	11
Sun Letters	11
Lesson 3: Greetings	12
Meaning of a schwa	14
Lesson 4: There is	15
Lesson 5: Not	16
The Tenween	16
Lesson 6: Verbs in command form	18
Lesson 7: Adjectives	19
Nouns precede adjectives in Arabic	19
Lesson 8: Adverbs	23
Verbs precede adverbs in Arabic	23
Lesson 9: Places	24
How questions are asked with intonation	24
Some Arabic Prefixes	25
Lesson 10: Traveling	26
Grammar	27
Summary of the 107 learned words in Part One excluding 600 cognates	27
Place short vowels & other symbols on learned words	31
Write these words in Arabic letters	33
Say your own sentences out of these learned patterns	35
Practice Quiz: Translate the learned lessons into Arabic	36
Four Major Arabic Dialects	39
Chart of the Learned Words in Four Arabic Dialects	40

Spoken Arabic for English Speakers

Part Two

Lesson 1: Verbs in command form 42

Lesson 2: I + verb 44

Learn these prepositions 47

The verbs "take" and "eat" conjugate differently 48

Lesson 3: He + verb 49

Lesson 4: We + verb 52

Lesson 5: She + verb 56

Lesson 6: You + verb 59

Lesson 7: You (feminine) + verb 63

Lesson 8: They + verb 67

Lesson 9: You (plural) + verb 70

Lesson 10: Future tense verbs 73

Past tense verbs 78

Summary of the 192 learned words in Part Two excluding 200 cognates 79

Place the short vowels (حَرَكات) and other Arabic symbols on Arabic text you learned 83

Write these words using Arabic letters, as in naam: نام 87

Say your own sentences or phrases out of these learned word 89

Practice Quiz: Translate the learned lessons into Arabic 92

Chart of verb conjugations 95

Chart of learned words in four major Arabic dialects 96

Chart of learned verbs in four major Arabic dialects 97

This is a college textbook, but it works for all ages and with or without a teacher. The author Camilia Sadik is a linguist, and she is a native-Arabic speaker. Sadik spent five long years dissecting Arabic, and she teaches Arabic college courses to English speakers. This book caters to the specific needs of English speakers. With the meticulous transliteration in this book, students begin to speak Arabic from the first day of class. The vowels, consonants, and nine Arabic symbols are dissected. The book contains 800+ cognates. No other methodology has 40+ original learning features in one program. It teaches sentence patterns, grouping of words, and conjugating of verbs. As a result, students learn a methodology to teach themselves to speak indefinitely. Each learned word is presented in four major Arabic dialects for students to choose their desired dialect. It is a class-tested approach. What's more is that the author dissected both Arabic and English; she teaches both languages in two different colleges in San Diego, California. You will also need to learn to read from *The Arabic Alphabet for English Speakers by Camilia Sadik*.

INTRODUCTION أَلْمُقَدِّمَة

Spoken Arabic for English Speakers

Instructions & Learning Notes

1. Direct Instructions: تعليمات أَلْكِتاب مَكْتوبَةً مُباشَرَةً في بِدايَة كُل دَرْس جَديد
Teachers do not need a teacher's guide because there are direct instructions before the start of each lesson in this entire book. All explanations are written in English, and the Arabic words are written both in Arabic letters and in English transliterations, as in (Madrid: med·reed′ مَدْريد). If any teacher doesn't agree with using transliteration, he or she has the choice of ignoring the transliteration and teaching only from the Arabic text available in this book. Some teachers insist on having a teacher's guide; and this long introduction is their teacher's guide.

2. Dots inside words, italic letters, stress marks: مَعْنى أَلْنقاط داخِل أَلْكَلِمات ومَعْنى أَلْحِروف أَلْمائِلَة وَعَلامَة أَلْتَشْديد
    1. All words in this book are divided into syllables as in, (radio: raad·yōo راديو).
    2. All silent letters are italicized like as in, (the rice: ′el·ruzz أَلْرُزّ).
    3. Stress marks are placed on every stressed syllable, as in (Cincinnati: sin·si·naa′·tee).

3. Understanding Arabic and English vowels is essential: فِهم حروف أَلْعِلَة أَلْعَرَبِيَة وَأَلْإِنْجِليزيَة مُهِم جداً
English vowels are a, e, i, o, u, sometimes y as in sky, and sometimes w as in few. Unlike Arabic, English uses the same letter for the short and for the long sound of a vowel. For instance, English uses the same letter "e" to represent the short ĕ sound as in "set" and the long ē sound as in "seat". Unlike English, Arabic has three letters for the long vowels and three distinct symbols for the short vowels. The short vowels are not letters; they are small strokes or blips written above or below the consonants; their name is He·re·kaat′ حَرَكات. Understanding the vowels in both languages is very necessary because vowels rule a language. Luckily, the author of this program dissected the vowels in both languages and has written books about them.

4. The three long Arabic vowels: أَلِف واو ياء
In this book, the three Arabic long vowels are represented in (aa أَلِف) that sound like the "a" in "cat", the (ee ياء) that sounds like the "ee" in "meet", and the (oo واو) that sounds like the "oo" in "boot".
    1. The ′elif: أَلِف
    The long Arabic vowel "aa" is called ′elif أَلِف and it is normally pronounced like the "a" in "father" but changes to like the "a" in "man" when next to an "emphatic" consonant. Emphatic consonants are: (H, A, D, S, Z حروف أَلْإِطْباق).
    The ′elif meqSooreh: أَلِف مَقْصورَة is a weaker version of the ′elif sound; it sounds like the English "aw" in "law" and it occurs only at the end of Arabic words. The symbol given to it in this book is "aw" as in music: mōo′·see·qaw: موسيقى.
    2. The waaw: واو
    The long vowel "oo" is called waaw واو and it sounds like the "oo" in "boot". In a few words, it sounds like the long vowel ō as in bōat. The few words are mainly derived from English or other foreign languages. Examples are: raad′·yōo, sti·ryōo′, te·li·fōon′, ′ōo′·fin,′el·bōom′, ′ōor·laan·dōo, ′ōo′·haa·yōo, dee′·trōoyt, dōo′·laar, bee′·yaa·nōo, te·le·fiz·yōon′, rōob, kaar′·tōon, shōo′·kōo·laa·taa, mōo′·see·qaw, meA·ke·rōo′·nee, bananas: mōoz موز, and plums: khōokh خوخ. It is said that the word (bananas: mōoz موز) is derived from the Persian language.
    3. The yaa′: ياء
    The long Arabic vowel "ee" is called yaa′ ياء and it is normally pronounced like the "ee" in "meet" but it stops being a vowel and it changes to the sound of "y"; when at the beginning of words or syllables, as in Japan: yaa·baan يابان.

Introduction

5. The three short Arabic vowels: فَتْحَة ضَمَة كَسْرَة

The three Arabic short vowels are represented in (e فَتْحَة) that sounds like the short English "e" in "set", (i كَسْرَة) that sounds like the short English "i" in "sit", and the (u ضَمَة) that sounds like the "u" in "put". The short Arabic vowels are not letters; instead, they are tiny blips or strokes written above or below consonants.

1. The fetHeh: فَتْحَة is represented with an "e" in this book, and it sounds like the short English vowel ĕ as in "set." When not stressed it sounds like a schwa, like the weak "e" sound in "brother". The fetHeh: فَتْحَة is not a letter but it is a blip written <u>above</u> consonants.
2. The Demeh: ضَمَة is a short vowel represented with a "u" in this book, and it sounds like the English "u" in "put". This Arabic short vowel has a strong sound, and it is also a blip written <u>above</u> consonants.
3. The kesreh: كَسْرَة is represented with an "i" in this book, and it sounds like short English vowel "i" in "sit". When stressed at the end of a word or a syllable, it sounds like the "i" in "ski." It is also a blip, but it is the only vowel written <u>below</u> the consonants.

6. Representing the fetHeh فَتْحَة sound with "e" not "a": تَرْجَمَة صَوت أَلْفَتْحَة

Too many Arabic words that contain the short Arabic vowel fetHeh فَتْحَة have been incorrectly transliterated or translated to English. The "e" should have been used, not the "a" to represent the sound of the Arabic fetHeh فَتْحَة. The prefix "Al", meaning "the" is widely used; it often prefixes Arabic proper nouns, especially names of places; an example is Al-Jazirah أَلْجَزِيرَة (Arabic: "The Island"). The "a", which is the fetHeh فَتْحَة should have been an "e" in Al-Jazirah because it sounds like a short English "e" not "a"; it should be spelled (El-Jezeereh). The precise sound of the fetHeh فَتْحَة is like the short English "e", not "a". In the beginning of her career, the author used "a" for the sound of the fetHeh فَتْحَة and her students would spell words like (thank you: shukr<u>a</u>n شُكْراً) as (shukr<u>aa</u>n شُكْران) confusing the "a" with the short vowel "a" in English.

7. Schwa صَوت حَرف أَلْعِلَة أَلضَعيف

A schwa is a name given to a weak sound of any English vowel. English dictionaries use an upside-down symbol to represent a schwa sound. A schwa sound is like the "a" sound in (begg**a**r). In Arabic, a schwa sound is like the second "e" sound in (fish: semek: سَمَك) It is usually the short Arabic vowels (e فَتْحَة) and (i كَسْرَة) that can sound like a schwa. The Arabic schwa is mainly represented by an "i" kesreh in Egyptian dialect (black: 'iswid: أَسْوِد) and by an "e" "fetHeh" in the Gulf dialect (black: 'eswed: أَسْوَد).

8. Six capital letters inside words: طاء، ضاد، عين، حاء، صاد، ظاء

Don't be discouraged when you see English capital letters inside words, as in ribaaT رباط. There aren't enough English letters to represent all the 28 Arabic letters; hence, six English capital letters are used to represent six Arabic sounds that do not have an equivalent letter sound in English. The capitol "T" represents the Arabic letter (Taa': طاء) as in (kilowatt: kee'·loo·waaT كيلو واط), a capital "D" represents the (Daad: ضاد) as in (Riyadh: ri·yaaD' رياض), a capital "A" represent the (Aeyn: عَين) as in (Ae·re·bee' عَرَبي), a capital "H" represent the (Haa': حاء) as in (He·bee'·bee حَبيبي), a capital "S" represents the (Saad: صاد) as in (bus: baaS باص) and a capital "Z" represents the (Zaa' ظاء) as in (meH·fooZ' مَحْفوظ).

1. T ط

    The capital "T" ط represents a slightly different sound of a "t." Examples of words that contain the "T" sound are (kilowatt: kee·lōo·waaT كيلو واط), (pants: ben·Te·loon بَنْطَلون), and (bottle: bu·Tul بُطُل), You will need to hear this Arabic sound to learn it.

2. A ع

    The capital "A" ع represents a slightly different sound from the English "a." Examples of words that contain "A" ع are (Saudi: si·Aoo·dee سعودي), (Iraq: Ai·raaq عِراق), and (street: shaa·riA شارع). You will need to hear this Arabic sound to learn it.

3. q ق

    The "q" قاف sounds slightly different from the English "k." Examples of words that contain "q" ق are (Iraq: Ai·raaq عراق), (hotel: fin·diq فِنْدِق), and (market: sooq سوق). You will need to hear this Arabic sound to learn it.

4. S ص

    The capital "S" ص represents a slightly different sound from the English "s"; it is close to the English "s" is "sum." Examples of words that contain the "S" صاد sound are (glass: klaaS كْلاص), (bus: baaS باص), (Somalia: 'el·Sōo·maal أَلصومال). You will need to hear this Arabic sound to learn it.

5. D ض

    The capital "D" ض represents a slightly different sound from the English "d." Examples of a word that contain the "D" sound are (eggs: beyD بَيض) and (white: 'eb·yeD أَبْيَض). You will need to hear this Arabic sound to learn it.

6. Z ظ

    The capital "Z" ظ represents a slightly different sound from the Arabic (D ض) and to many Arabic speakers, it is difficult to tell their sounds apart. The good news is that the Z occurs in about 38 words. In Egyptian dialect, this difficultly is solved because a plain "z" sound is used to represent this sound. Examples of words that contain the (Zaa' ظاء) sound are (meH·fooZ' مَحْفوظ), (clean: ne·Zeef نَظيف), (great: Ae·Zeem' عَظيم) and the letter (Zaa' ظاء).

9. (dh ذ) and (th ث)

In this book, the (th ث) symbol is equivalent to the sound of (th ث) as in (thermos: thir·mus ثِرمُس) and the (dh ذ) is equivalent to the sound of (dh ذ) as in (Heather: he·dher هَذّر).

10. There are no letters equivalent to p, v, o, ch, hard g, and si:

Arabic does not have letters equivalent to the English p, v, long ō, ch as in chips, hard g, and si as in television. However, Arabic speakers may say the "p" in "piano" and write (bee·yaa·nōo بيانو). Similarly, Arabic speakers may say the "v" in "oven" and write ('ōo·fin أوفِن). They may say the "ch" in "chips" and write (jibs جِبْس). They may say the hard "g" in "garage" and write (ka·raaj گَراج). They do say the long "ō" sound in "radiō" and write (raad·yoo راديو). Arabic uses the "z" for the "si" sound as in (television: ta·la·fiz·yōon تَلَفِزيون) and they do that both in spoken and in written Arabic.

11. Stressed syllable: أَلْمَقْطَع ٱلْمُشَدَد

A syllable that contains any of the three long Arabic vowels (aa, oo, ee) attracts the stress to itself, as in (Beirut: bey·root'), (chair: kur·see'), and (book: ki·taab'). Otherwise, Arabic words are normally stressed on the first syllable, as in (sugar: suk'·kar).

1. Stress marks: عَلامَة أَلْتَشْديد موجودة في كَلِمات أَلْكِتاب كُلّها

    A stress mark is placed at the end of each stressed syllable in all the words in this book, as in: (fe·laa'·fil فَلافِل).

2. A rule to know the stress in a syllable: قاعدة أَلْتَشْديد عَلى أَلْمَقْطَع

    This is a concrete simple rule to place a stress mark on a syllable. The stress is on the first long vowel in a word, as in (physics: feez'·yaa' فيزْياء). If there is no long vowel in a word the stress is on the first syllable, as in (sugar: suk'·ker سُكَّر).

12. hem'·zeh هَمْزَة as in (physics: feez'·yaa' فيزياء):

The name of this symbol is hem'·zeh هَمْزَة and it sounds like the sound of the glottal stop in the English word 'Uh 'Oh! It is most known in Arabic as the letter that rides on long vowels. The English symbol given to the hemzeh هَمْزَة in this book is an apostrophe, as in 'e·laa·skeh ألاسْكا. There is an ongoing debate whether the hamzah هَمْزَة is or is not a letter. However, it may be considered a letter when it can stand alone, as in (physics: feez'·yaa' فيزياء). The rest of the time, the hemzeh هَمزَة occurs riding on the long vowels and thus it may not be considered a letter. When the hemzeh rides on the long vowels, it suppresses their sounds; it makes them silent and then we only hear the hemzeh هَمزَة sound. The followings are the hemzeh هَمزَة positions alone and when riding above or below the three long Arabic vowels like this أ, إ, و and ي. There is a long-detailed chapter about the hemzeh in *The Arabic Alphabet for English Speakers by Camilia Sadik*.

13. The silent 'elif under the hemzeh: أَلِف صامِتِة تحت أَلهَمزَة
Whenever you see an 'e أ at the beginning of a word or a syllable, it is spelled with a silent (aa أ) before it. For instance, (food: 'ekl أكل) is spelled aa'ekl أكل and the 'el as in 'el·Hi·saab is spelled (aa'el·Hi·saab أَلحِساب) in Arabic. The hemzeh rides on the 'elif and it suppresses its sound.

14. Sun Letters: أَلحِروف أَلشَمسِيَة
Fifteen of the Arabic letters are called Sun Letters, and they are:
سين، شين، صاد، راء، تاء، طاء، لام، جيم، نون، دال، ذال، ثاء، زاي، ضاد، ظاء.

t ت	r ر	S ص	sh ش	s س
d د	n ن	j ج	l ل	T ط
Z ظ	D ض	z ز	th ث	dh ذ

15. Silent L ل before a sun letter: أَللام الصامت قبل الحرف الشمسي
The "l" in 'el أَل becomes silent when followed by a sun letter, as in ('el·soob أَلسوب), ('el·shaay أَلشاي), ('el·Se·HeeH أَلصحيح), ('el·ruzz أَلرُزّ), ('el·tek·see أَلتَكسي), ('el·Taa·lib أَلطالِب), ('el·le·dheed أَللذيذ), ('el·je·meel أَلجَميل), ('el·naas أَلناس), ('el·di·jaaj أَلدجاج), ('el·dhe·heb أَلذَهَب), ('el·thoom أَلثوم), ('el·zee·braa أَلزيبرا), ('el·De·meh أَلضَمَة), and ('el·Zaa' أَلظاء). If not followed by a sun letter, the 'e in 'el is silent and the "l" has a sound, as in ('el·baab أَلباب) and as in 'el plus any other letter that is not a sun letter, including the vowels ('el·'oo·fin أَلأوفِن).

16. No vowel sound: sikoon سِكون
The word si·koon' سِكون literally means "no sound." The sikoon سِكون is a tiny circle written above a letter to assert the no vowel existence, as it being above the (d دْ). When there is no vowel between two consonants, there can be a (sikoon سِكون), as in (film: film فِلم). Sometimes, a sikoon can be at the end of words, as in (mother: 'um أُم). What English calls a consonant blend; Arabic calls it a sikoon سِكون. Examples of sikoon in words are: (Madrid: med·reed' مَدْريد) and (food: 'ekl أَكل).

17. Double consonants: sheddeh شَدَّة
The shed'·deh شَدَّة is a tiny symbol that goes above a consonant to assert the existence of a double consonant, as in (rice: ruzz رُزّ). Instead of doubling the consonants, the sheddeh شَدَّة is placed on the consonant and takes the place of the second consonant.

18. Short vowel ă meddeh مَدَّة: آ as in (Adam: آدَم)
The med'·deh مَدَّة is a symbol that sits above the 'elif أَلِف and together they sound like the English short vowel "a", like the first "a" in (Adam: آدَم) and as in (Ann آن). It also occurs inside words at the beginning of a syllables, as in (Koran قُرآن). The meddeh مَدَّة occurs at the beginning of words or syllables and it is a minor symbol because it is in a limited number of words.

19. The feminine suffix (eh ﺔ) or (et ﺔ) أَلتاء أَلمَربوطَة
Most countries and cities' names are expressed in a feminine gender. Most of which end in the suffix (et ﺔ). This suffix is written with an "et" but pronounced "eh". i.e., The (et ﺔ) is pronounced (eh ﺔ) as in (Syria: sooryet سوريَة), sounding like (Syria: sooryeh سورْيَة). The Arabic words for "country" is (dewleh

دَوْلَة) and city is (medeeneh مَدينة) and both end with (et ة) that sounds like (eh ه). Both words are in a feminine form. Think of a country's name being feminine as mother earth. The suffix is pronounced as (eh ه) or (et ة) depending on the word that follows it or if it isn't followed by any words. When it's followed by an owner, it is pronounced like "et" as in: (Sam being the owner of a car: siy·yaa·ret Sam). There is more about the taa' merbooTeh أَلْتاء أَلْمَربوطة that is explained in the book titled *The Arabic Alphabet for English Speakers* by Camilia Sadik.

20. The tenween تَنْوين as in شُكْراً:
The ten·ween' تَنْوين is an ending (suffix) that can have three different sounds. The first sound is like the "en" as in "taken" and in the Arabic word (thank you: shuk·ren شُكْراً). The other two sounds are "un" that sounds like the "un" in (a book: ki·taa·bun كِتابٌ) and the "in" sound as in (ki·taa·bin كِتابٍ). The "un" and "in" endings involve the grammatical structure of sentences, not just words. It is best to study them in advanced levels of Arabic in the future. In this book, we are mainly concerned with the grammar inside the words and in simple sentences. Hence, "en" ending as in shuk·ren شُكْراً is the only one we will be studying here. When first hearing the "en" sound as in شُكْراً, one assumes that it is spelled with an "n ن." However, there is no "n ن" in these tenween endings. Instead, there is a double blip sitting above the 'elif as in shuk·ren شُكْراً or above the end isolated hemzeh like this ء as in (please: ri·jaa''en رجاءً). Notice that most of these words are adverbs. Learn the tenween in these words:

thanks	shuk'·raaen	شُكْراً
you're welcome	Aef·waaen	عَفْواً
very	ji·daaen	جداً
please (not v.)	ri·jaa''en	رجاءً
a lot	ke·thee·raaen	كَثيراً
in the morning	Se·baa·Haaen	صَباحاً
always	daa·'i·maaen	دائِماً
in the evening	me·saa·aa'en	مَساءً
nighttime	ley·laaen	لَيلاً
a little	qe·lee·laaen	قَليلاً
first of all	'ew·we·laaen	أوَلاً

21. Summary of the Arabic vowels and other symbols:

de: دَ	daa: دا	du: دُ	doo: دو
di: دِ	dee: دي	-den: دً	dd: دّ
dl: دْ	aw: ى	ă=aa: آ	': ء

22. Right to left: كِتابَة أَلْعَرَبِية وَقِراءَتَها مِن أَلْيَسار إلى أَلْيَمين
Arabic is written and read from right to left←.

23. Cursive only: أَلْحِروف أَلْعَرَبِيَة مُتَصِلَة (مَرْج)
Arabic is written only in cursive; even in print, Arabic is in cursive. Like the English cursive, Arabic letters are connected to each other. However, six of the Arabic letters are not connected to each other but they are connected to other letters from their right side only. They are selfish letters because they receive connection, but they do not give it; they connect to the preceding but not to the following letters.

24. Unique transliteration: كِتابَة أَلْعَرَبِيَة بِحِروف إنْجِليزِيَة
Using transliteration in this book is one choice; the other choice is using the Arabic letters that are also available in this book, and they are written next to the transliteration. Transliteration in this book looks like this te·li·foon' تَلِفون. The author transferred the Arabic alphabet to English letters. Using transliteration, students begin to speak Arabic from the first day of class. They also learn the 28 Arabic letters and the nine symbols within weeks. Transliteration is only a step and when finishing with this book and the alphabet book, students will directly read any other Arabic text.

25. Meticulous sounds' translation: دِقَة تَرْجَمَة أَلْصَوْت وَالْألِف أَلْمَقْصورة كَمَثَّل
Arabic sounds are meticulously translated; it took the author five long years discovering and class testing to produce two unique books; see how the English "aw" as in "law" is introduced for the first time ever to represent the sound of ى as in moo'·see·qaw: موسيقى.

26. Intonation: بالعامية، نسأل السؤال بتغيير اللكنة
In spoken Arabic, questions are asked by changing the voice to a questioning tone (intonation), with no change in the word order. When writing, simply add a question mark: (you want tea? تريد شاي؟).

27. No "a" and no "is": هَذا راديو
Arabic does not use the articles "a" or "an" before a noun. In Arabic, "a radio" would be "radio" "raad·yoo راديو." The "this" in Arabic means "this is" without the "is." For example, "This is a radio." would be (this radio: haa·dhaa raad·yoo هَذا راديو).

28. In Arabic, nouns precede adjectives: الأسِم قَبل الصِفة
"a good rice" is expressed (rice good: ruzz kweyyis رُزّ كوَيِّس). Similarly, "a white house" is expressed (house white: beyt 'ebyeD بَيت أَبْيَض). In Arabic, there is no "is" and "big door" can be expressed:
- the door is big/ the door big: ('elbaab kebeer أَلْباب كَبير).
- the door is big/ the door it is big: ('elbaab huwe kebeer أَلْباب هو كَبير).
- the specific door that is big: (the door the big: أَلْباب أَلْكَبير).
- any door a door is big / door big: باب كَبير

29. Verbs precede adverbs: أَلْفِعل يَسْبِق أَلْظَرف
Just like English, verbs come before adverbs in Arabic. It makes sense to have the verbs first because adverbs describe these verbs. Example: (Sam drives fast: Sam yesooq bisurAeh سام يسوق بِسُرْعَة)

30. In this book, all verbs are first introduced in a masculine gender and in a command form: (you male go to sleep: naam نام) and then they are conjugated and used in sentence patterns. When you ask Arabic speakers for the meaning of a verb, they immediately tell you the masculine form of that verb in the present tense. For instance, you ask them for the meaning of "sleep" or "to sleep". There answer is usually (he sleeps: yenaam يَنام). Ask them for the command form of that verb so you will know how to conjugate it.

31. At the end of this book, there is a chart of all the learned verbs and the way they conjugate, like this:

I: 'enaa أنا	He: huwe هُوَ	We: neHnu نَحْنُ	She: hiye هَيَ	You: 'inte إنْتَ	You: 'inti إنْتِ	They: hum هُم
'enaam	yenaam	nenaam	tenaam	tenaam	tenaami	yenaamoon
'ejeeb	yejeeb	nejeeb	tejeeb	tejeeb	tejeebi	yejeeboon
'eshoof	yeshoof	neshoof	teshoof	teshoof	teshoofi	yeshoofoon
'erooH	yerooH	nerooH	terooH	terooH	terooHi	yerooHoon

32. The prefix (the: 'el أَلْـ)
The *aa'el* أَلْـ means "the" and it is a prefix in Arabic, as in (the door: 'elbaab أَلْبَاب) Being a prefix means it attaches to the word that follows it. The *aa'el* أَلْـ can mean "the" and it can simply be a part of a person's surname or a part of a country's name. Some countries' names like (Algeria: أَلْجَزَائِر) begin with *aa'el*, some can't take an *aa'el* like (Palestine: فَلَسْطِين), and others may take an *aa'el* أَلْـ only to mean "the" (The Gulf: أَلْخَلِيج). The 'elif أ in *aa'el* أَلْـ is silent because the hemzeh هَمْزَة riding on it suppresses its sound.

33. The (this: haa·dhaa هَذَا) pronounced like the prefix (he هَـ)
The word (this: haadhaa هَذَا) followed by ('el + sun letter) is pronounced like (he هَـ), as in he·soob هَسوب, he·shaay هَشَاي, he·Se·boon هَصَابون, he·ruzz هَرُزّ, he·tek·see هَتَكْسِي, he·Taa·lib هَطَالِب, he·leHm هَلَحْم, he·jaa·keyt هَجَاكِيت, he·naas هَنَاس, he·di·jaaj هَدِجَاج, he·dhe·heb هَذَهَب, he·thoom هَثوم, he·zee·braa هَزيبرا, he·De·meh هَضَمَة, he·Zaa' هَظَاء. If not followed by a sun letter, haa·dhaa + 'el becomes hel, as in (hel·baab هَلْبَاب) and (hel·'ōo·fin هَلْأُوفِن).

34. The prefix (and: we وَ) pronounced (wi وِ):
(w**e** + 'el + sun letter) sound like (wi + 'el + sun letter) as in (and the rice: we'elruzz وَرُزّ) sounding like (wiruzz وِرُزّ). But, (we + 'el + other than a sun letter) sounds like (wil) as in the change from (we'elbaab وَلبَاب) to (wilbaab وِلبَاب).

35. Arabic prefixes: أَلْبَادِئَات فِي أَلْعَرَبِيَة
It saves space on a page to have many prefixes in Arabic. Here are a few examples:
  1. and: we-: وَ as in (and sugar: wesukker وَسُكَّر)
  2. the: 'el-: أَلْـ as in (the book: 'elkitaab إِلْكِتَاب)
  3. to: li- لِـ as in: (to Baghdad: libeghdaad لِبَغْدَاد)
  4. to the: lil- لِلْـ as in (lilsooq لِلْسُوق)
     These are in spoken, not formal Arabic:
  5. from the: min + 'el = mnil- مْنِل as in (from the market: mnilsooq مْنِل سوق)
  6. this: hel- هَلْـ: as in (this book: helkitaab هَلْكِتَاب)

36. Spelling: تَهَجِي
  1. When you see ('el أَلْـ) at the beginning of a word or syllable, it is spelled with a silent (aa أَلِف) before it. For instance, 'ekl is actually spelled *aa*'ekl أَكْل with a silent (aa أَلِف) before it. The hemzeh هَمْزَة that rides on top of the 'elif tends to suppress the sound of 'elif. Another example is ('elHisaab أَلْحِسَاب) that is spelled (*aa*'elHisaab) with a silent 'elif before it (أَلْحِسَاب).
  2. When you see the word "this" that means "haadhaa", it is spelled hedhaa هَذَا.
  3. When you see the word "but" that means "laakin", it is spelled "lekin" أَكِن.

37. About this Teaching Methodology: عَن طَرِيقَة أَلتَعلِيم فِي هَذَا أَلْكِتَاب
It is rare for a teacher to have dissected both Arabic and English. The developer of this unique teaching/learning methodology is a native-Arabic speaker, and she spent five long years dissecting Arabic and then 15 more years dissecting English.

38. The value of learning sentence patterns vs. fixed sentences: تعلُّم نَمَاذج الجُمَل غَير مَحْدود
Learning sentence patterns, you can say an unlimited number of sentences. You may say hundreds of sentences with one learned sentence pattern. However, learning only one fixed sentence at a time, one is limited to those few sentences only. This explains the reason people say a few fixed sentences and then stop, and they may never speak again. Saying "hello" and "goodbye", etc. is very limited.

39. Following instructions: أَهَمِيَة إتِباع تَعليمات أَلْكِتاب
Teachers need to warn students that this easy method is different and true learning relies immensely on following instruction and following the four simple learning steps explained before each lesson. Lessons are introduced step-by-step, and they are cumulative; each lesson adds more to the previous ones.

40. Unique learning methodology: طَريقَة تَعْليم فَريدَة مِن نَوعِها
Over 30 learning techniques are used to make learning easy and possible: Newly discovered rules followed by immediate practice to learn the Arabic vowels, the consonants, consonant blends, double letters, schwa, the Arabic hemzeh, how to divide Arabic words into syllables, which syllables to be stressed, silent letters, and a one of its kind learning methodology that requires no forced memorization or flash cards.

Sample Rule: Arabic words are normally stressed on the first long vowel in a word, as in (Baghdad: begh·daad'·بَغْداد) and as in (Denmark: de·nee'·maark دَنيمارْك). If a word doesn't contain a long vowel, it is stressed on the first short vowel, as in (Damascus: di'·meshq دِمَشْق).

41. Grouping of words: تَجْميع أَلْكَلِمات أَلْمُتَشابِهَة سَوِيَة
All words of a similar pattern are grouped together, divided into syllables, each silent letter is *italicized*. The words are prepared for the students to simply read and learn. Unlike traditional teaching that presents students with one or a few examples, the author collects 10 to 30 examples or more and hands them to students.

42. Class-tested, effective approach: طَريقَة أَلْتَعْليم فَعالة وهي مُجَرَبَة في أَرْبَع جامِعات أَمْريكِيَة
Professor Camilia Sadik class-tested her methodology while teaching English speakers in four colleges in San Diego, California. With this class-tested, effective approach to learning, most master the Arabic alphabet in fifteen or thirty days, learning either one or two letters per day.

43. Specifically for English speakers: تَعْليم أَلْعَرَبِيَة هنا هُوَ تَحديداً لمتكلمي اَلإنْجليزية
Using both books by *Camilia Sadik*, students begin to speak Arabic from the first day of class. Students begin to read immediately using English transliteration, and reading aloud enables them to speak Arabic from the first day of class. This program caters to the specific needs of English speakers, and it is comprehensive; it covers all aspects of Arabic relevant to a new learner.

44. A book for all: كِتاب لِكافَة أَلأعمار وَأَلْمُسْتَوَيات مَعَ مُعَلِّم أَو بِدون مُعَلِّم
Students may learn from this book with or without a teacher. This book also accommodates diverse needs in one classroom. English speakers from multilevel, multicultural backgrounds and from any age group can learn to speak, read, and write in Arabic in one classroom. Not only do students learn, but also, they remember what they learn. Students retain what they learn without forced memorization, but through logical explanations and reading the practice lessons aloud.

45. More features: مَزيد مِن أَلْمَزايا
This book is easy to read, the language is in plain, spoken Arabic. The English transliteration used is very precise and consistent when it corresponds to each Arabic sound. All short vowels and other Arabic symbols are written above or below Arabic letters. This book is in large print. See a complete chart of the alphabet at the end of the alphabet book. Notice the silent letters being italicized, words being divided into syllables, the stressed syllables marked with a stress mark. See the consistency of sound corresponding in the following examples:

Cincinnati:	sin·si·naa'·tee	سِنْسِناتي
Beirut:	bey'·root	بَيْروت
falafel:	fe·laa'·fil	فَلافِل

Spoken Arabic for English Speakers

kabob:	ke·baab'	كَباب
the market:	'il·sooq'	إلسوق
in English:	bi·'el·'in·ki·lee·zee	بألإنكِليزي

46. The four learning steps in this book: أربَع خَطَوات لِتَعليم ألدَرس
    ❶ Learning Step One: Read aloud to memorize the new words.
    ❷ Learning Step Two: Learn the new sentence pattern.
    ❸ Learning Step Three: Say as many sentences as you can remember, using old and new patterns.
    ❹ Learning Step Four: Write as many sentences as you can remember.

47. Learning Step Three is Essential: ألخِطوَة ألثالِثَة مُهِمَة جِداً
In this step students close their books and speak aloud with new and old sentence patterns. This is the learning step that contributes to speaking fluency by creating your own sentences. If any teacher tends to go over Step Three to learn sentence patterns too fast, students may stop to ask the teachers to slow down. Much more time needs to be spent on this step.

48. Instructions to follow rigorously in Learning Step Three: تَعليمات لتَطبيق ألخِطوَة ألثالِثَة
    1. If in a classroom, students need to quickly break into groups of two, take a few minutes to speak, not in a question-and-answer form, but one student may speak while the other listens only, and then rotate several times until fluency is achieved.
    2. Corrections during speech are not permitted. If you need more corrections, go back to previous steps. If any student or anyone tries to correct you during speech, tell them please do not correct me because that will make me lose confidence and I may not speak again.
    3. Avoid thinking about correct grammar when you speak because that will divert your thoughts from speaking to using grammar. Focus only on fluency. Don't worry if you make grammatical mistakes, you learn best from hearing your own mistakes.
    4. Focus on "what" is being said, not on "how" things are said.
    5. Free yourself from worrying about making grammatically perfect sentences; you will achieve that naturally and without you realizing it.
    6. Speak only Arabic in this step and stay in Arabic. If you say anything in English, you'll need to stop and start over.
    7. Use this step to develop the ability to obliterate hesitation, saying "How do you say," and vacillating during speech.
    8. If you wish to produce complex sentences, focus on the simple ones. Complex ones come as a natural result without you trying to force them. Like children learning to speak, simple sentences are combined in the brain and then complex ones are produced naturally, without children trying to produce them.
    9. Be very LOUD and use this step as an opportunity to develop your fluency, confidence, and memory.
    10. Do not stop speaking until you achieve fluency.
    11. If you find yourself studying but not learning, it is because you aren't reading aloud, and you aren't following the rest of the directions given to you in this book. This new memorization method works only if all the instructions given to you are followed rigorously. If you read silently you will understand, but you will not speak. You cannot retain even a perfect sentence unless your mouth utters it. So, if you haven't read aloud, it is not too late. Go back and read again aloud☞.

49. Why should you read and speak aloud: أهَمِيَة ألقِراءَة بِصَوت عالٍ
    1. To hear your own mistakes and learn from them.

2. To hear sound and improve your pronunciation.
3. To practice alone, you don't have to have another person listening to you.
4. To gain confidence and fluency in speaking, reading, and then writing.
5. To have this class-tested methodology work for you.
6. Because more memory comes from using more senses, as in hearing the sounds.
7. Because this method is different, and it doesn't work without uttering the sounds.
8. Because it's not enough to think a sentence, you need to say it.
9. Because speaking a language is about making sounds.

50. About the Arabian Culture: عَن ٱلتُّراث ٱلْعَرَبِي
Repetition in the Arabian culture means assertion: ٱلتكرار يَدل على ٱلإصرار في التراث ٱلْعَرَبِي
As in these examples, certain words are repeated to manifest how Arabic speakers tend to repeat to express assertion:
   Is there soup: fee soop? في سوب؟
   There is, there is, the soup is plenty plenty: fee, fee 'el·soob ketheer ketheer. في، في، إلْسوب كثير كثير.
   Always there is soup, always: daa·'i·men fee soob, daa·'i·men. دائماً في سوب ، دائماً.

51. Typically, polite words like "thank you" "you're welcome" and "please" are not excessively used among friends and family members. If one were to continue to use them, his or her close friends and family members might say, "What is wrong?" Excessive use of such words is not very desired because some may view that to escape paying back the favor. Also, such words are normally used in formal settings, not among real friends. Friends don't thank each other in words. Instead, they wait for the opportunity to give something back in return. Usually, Arabian mentality tends to view excessive use of such words as an attempt to put walls among friends, and sometimes they see the person that overuses these words as a salesperson. Of course, not every Arabian country in the Middle East has this exact same culture. For instance, this is truer in the Gulf area and less true in Egypt, Syria, and Lebanon wherein many survive on tourism and must use such polite words as they entertain tourists.

52. Different Arabic Dialects: إِخْتِلاف ٱللُّهجات ٱلْعَرَبِيَة
Among the various dialects, words may be pronounced differently and sometimes a completely different word is used in different countries. For instance, "now" in FuSHaw ٱلْفُصْحى is ('elaan ٱلآن), in Egyptian it is (dil·we'·tee دِلْوَءْتِ), in Lebanese it is (hel·laa هَلا), and in Iraqi is (he·seh هَسَه). At the end of part one and part two of this book, there are charts of all the learned words in the four major dialects, including the (FuSHaw فُصْحى).

53. The Four Major Arabic Dialects: ٱللَّهَجات ٱلْعَرَبِية ٱلْأربَعَة ٱلرَّئيسِيَة
Arabic speakers in 22 Arabian countries speak a countless number of dialects. In addition to the formal form of Arabic (فُصْحى), there are three other major dialects spoken in three major regions in the Middle East, and they are:
   1. The Egyptian dialect ٱللَّهَجَة ٱلْمَصْرِيَة
   2. The Gulf area dialect ٱللَّهَجَة الخَلِيجِيَة
   3. The Mediterranean dialect لَهْجَة دِوَل ٱلْبَحْر ٱلأبْيَض ٱلْمُتَوَسِط

54. The Egyptian Dialect: ٱللَّهَجَة ٱلْمَصْرِيَة
The Egyptian dialect is the most understood in all Arabian countries. This is due to the movie industry that flourished in Egypt since the 1950s and Arabic speakers watched Egyptian movies and they still do. If one is trying to learn spoken Arabic, it is safer to learn the Egyptian dialect. In this spoken Arabic book, the author picked the words that are most understood in every Arabian country, mostly Egyptian dialect is used. At the end of Part One and Part Two of this book, there are charts of the learned words

presented the four major dialects. From the charts, you may select words you wish to learn from any of the four dialects.

55. A list of the Arabian countries and their capitols: ألدِوَل ألعَرَبِيَة وَعَواصِمَها
    1. Gulf region: ألدِوَل الخَليجِيَة
       Iraq: ألعِراق →Baghdad: بَغْداد   Kuwait: ألكُوَيت→Kuwait: ألكُوَيت
       Saudi Arabia: ألسِعوديَة →Riyadh: ألرياض   Bahrain: ألبَحرَين →Manama: ألمَنامَة
       Oman: عُمان →Muscat: مَسقَط   UAE: ألإمارات → Abu Dhabi: أبو ظَبي
       Dubai: دُبَي →Dubai: دُبَي   Qatar: قَطَر → Doha: ألدوحَة
    2. The Mediterranean region: دِوَل ألبَحر ألأبيَض ألمُتَوَسِط
       Lebanon: لُبنان →Beirut: بَيْروت   Syria: سوريَة →Damascus: دِمَشق
       Jordan: ألأردُن →Amman: عَمّان   Palestine: فِلسطين →Jerusalem: ألقُدْس
       Yemen: ألَيَمَن →Sana: صَنْعاء   Aden: عَدَن →Aden: عَدَن
    3. Egypt and Parts of Africa: ألدِوَل ألقَريبة من مِصر
       Egypt: مِصر →Cairo: ألقاهِرَة   Libya: ليبيا → Tripoli: طَرَبلُس
       Tunisia: تونِس →Tunis: تونِس   Algeria: ألجَزائِر →Algeria: ألجَزائِر
       Morocco: ألمَغْرِب →Rabat: ألرباط   Sudan: ألسودان →Khartoum: ألخَرْطوم
       Somalia: ألصومال →Mogadishu: مَقْديشو   Djibouti: جيبوتي →Djibouti: جيبوتي
       Mauritania: موريتانيا →Nouakchott: نَواكُشوط

56. In this book, you can choose your dialect from the charts at end of each section in this book. You may choose your dialect and plug in the words chosen to use in the lessons. These are two slices of such charts to show how they are listed:

Learned Words in the Four Major Dialects

Learned Word	Egypt	Mediterranean	Gulf	FuSHaw
haa·dhaa هَذا	daa دا	hey·dhaa هَيْدا	haa·dhaa هَذا	haa·dhaa هَذا
sooq سوق	soo' سوء	soo' سوء	sook سوك	sooq سوق
kitaab كِتاب	ki·taab كِتاب	kitaab كِتاب	kitaab كِتاب	ki·taab كِتاب
shu·baak شُباك	shi·baak شِباك	shi·baak شِباك	shu·baak شُباك	shu·baak شُباك
'elaan ألآن	dil we·'e·tee دِلْوَءْتي	he·laa هَلا	he·seh هَسَه	'el·aan ألآن

Learned Verbs in Four Major Arabic Dialects

Learned Verbs	Egyptian	Medittariane	Gulf	FuSHa
yenaam يَنام	yinaam يِنام	yenaam يَنام	yenaam يَنام	yenaam يَنام
yejeeb يَجيب	yigeeb يِكيب	yejeeb يَجيب	yejeeb يَجيب	yejlub يَجْلُب
yeshoof يَشوف	yishoof يِشوف	yeshoof يَشوف	yeshoof يَشوف	yeraw يَرى
yerooH يَروح	yirooH يِروح	yerooH يَروح	yerooH يَروح	yedhheb يَذْهَب
yesewwee يَسَوّي	yiAmil يَعْمِل	yesaawwee يَساوي	yesewwee يَسَوّي	yeAmel يَعْمَل
yimshee يَمْشي	yimshee يِمْشي	yimshee يِمْشي	yimshee يِمْشي	yemshee يَمْشي

Books by the Author Camilia Sadik كُتُب المؤلفة كاميليا صادق

Arabic Books: كُتُب بالعربية للمؤلفة

1. *Spoken Arabic for English Speakers*: This book teaches spoken Arabic to beginners.
2. *Arabic Alphabet for English Speakers*: This book teaches the 28 Arabic letters and nine symbols.
3. *English for Arabic Speakers*: This book teaches spoken English to Arabic speakers. However, it's a great resource for English speakers to learn commonly spoken Arabic words in both languages. For instance, chapter one lists all the items that are in a home both in Arabic and in English.

➤ *The Arabic Alphabet for English Speakers*: كتاب الحروف الأبجدية لمتكلمي الإنكليزية

This is a college textbook, but it works for all ages. You will need this book to learn to read and write in Arabic while you are learning to speak. This book caters to the specific needs of English speakers. With the meticulous transliteration, students begin to read Arabic from the first day of class. 800+ cognates are used. The vowels, consonants, and nine Arabic symbols are dissected. The essential rules that govern the structure of Arabic letters are discovered. No other methodology has 40+ original learning features in one program. Each letter is dissected and explained. This is a class-tested approach, for all ages, and it works with or without a teacher. What's more is that the author professor Sadik is a linguist who dissected both English and Arabic.

English Books: كُتُب بالإنكليزية للمؤلفة

1. *Read Instantly*: This book teaches English phonics to English speakers.
2. *Learn to Spell 500 Words a Day*: Each vowel is in a volume and consonants are in a volume.
3. *100 Spelling Rules*: It contains 100+ English spelling rules discovered by the author.
4. All the Compound Words: It contains nearly all the English compound words.

About the Author: عن المؤلفة

The author, Camilia Sadik is a linguist, and she simultaneously teaches both English and Arabic in two different community colleges in San Diego, California. She spent five long years dissecting Arabic and fifteen additional years dissecting English.

Offering Intense Courses: دروس خِصوصِيَة لِلْطَلَبَة أو لِلْمُعَلِمين

The author Camilia Sadik or her representative offer intense workshops worldwide. The workshop may be a day or several days to teach reading and spelling in English, and to teach spoken Arabic and the Arabic Alphabet. The workshops may be for students or to train the trainers.

Visit our Arabic website: EnglishForArabicSpeakers.com
Visit our English website: SpellingRules.com
Email us: spell@spellingrules.com

Worldwide Copyright

WARNING: Copyright © by Camilia Sadik 2023. All rights are reserved. No part of this publication may be reproduced or distributed in any form or by any means. Teacher may not copy any pages or ideas from this book to distribute to students. Please note that these books are for sale at a discounted rate, whereby teachers and students each uses a copy to teach or to learn.

حقوق الطبع محفوظة للمؤلفة كاميليا صادق منذ عام 2023

PART ONE

Important Learning Notes

1. Right to left: كِتابَة أَلْعَرَبية من أَلْيَسار إَلى أَلْيَمين
Arabic is written and read from right to left←.

2. No capital letters: لا توجَد حِروف كَبيرَة بِالعَرَبيَة
There are no capital letters (uppercase) in Arabic.

3. Cursive only: (مَزج) أَلْحروف أَلْعَرَبيَة مُتَصِلَة
Arabic is written only in cursive; even in print, Arabic is in cursive. Like the English cursive, Arabic letters are connected to each other. However, six of the Arabic letters are not connected to each other but they are connected to other letters from their right side only. They are selfish letters because they receive connection, but they do not give it; they connect to the preceding but not to the following letters.

4. Dots inside words, italic letters, stress marks: مَعْنى أَلْنقاط داخِل أَلْكَلِمات ومَعنى أَلْحِروف أَلْمائِلَة وَعَلامَة أَلْتَّشْديد
   1. All words in this book are divided into syllables as in, (radio: raad·yōo راديْو).
   2. All silent letters are italicized like as in, (the rice: 'el·ruzz أَلْرُزّ).
   3. Stress marks are placed on every stressed syllable, as in (Cincinnati: sin·si·naa'·tee).

5. Six capital letters inside words: طاء، ضاد، عين، حاء، صاد، ظاء
There are six English capital letters used in this book to represent six of the Arabic letters that do not have an equivalent letter sound in English. The capitol "T" represents the Arabic letter Taa': طاء as in (kilowatt: kee'·loo·waaT كيلو واط), a capital "D" represents the Daad: ضاد as in (Riyadh: ri·yaaD' رياض), a capital "A" represent the Aeyn: عَين as in (Arabic: Ae·re·bee' عَرَبي), a capital "H" represent the Haa': حاء as in (He·bee'·bee حَبيبي), a capital "S" represents the Saad: صاد as in (bus: baaS باص), and a capital "Z" represents the Zaa' ظاء as in (meH·fooZ' مَحْفوظ).

6. There are no letters equivalent to p, v, o, ch, hard g, and si:
Arabic does not have letters equivalent to the English p, v, long ō, ch as in chips, hard g, and si as in television. However, Arabic speakers may say the "p" in "piano" and write (bee·yaa·nōo بيانو). Similarly, Arabic speakers may say the "v" in "oven" and write ('ōo·fin أوفِن). They may say the "ch" in "chips" and write (jibs جِبْس). They may say the hard "g" in "garage" and write (ka·raaj گَراج). They do say the long "ō" sound in "radiō" and write (raa·dyoo راديو). Arabic uses the "z" for the "si" sound as in (television: ta·la·fiz·yōon تَلَفِزيون) and they do that both in spoken and in written Arabic.

7. Understanding Arabic and English vowels is essential: فِهم حروف أَلْعِلَة أَلْعَرَبيَة وَأَلْإِنْجِليزيَة مُهِم جداً
English vowels are a, e, i, o, u, sometimes y as in sky, and sometimes w as in few. Unlike Arabic, English uses the same letter for the short and for the long sound of a vowel. For instance, English uses the same letter "e" to represent the short ĕ sound as in "set" and the long ē sound as in "seat". Unlike English, Arabic has three letters for the long vowels and three distinct symbols for the short vowels. The short vowels are not letters; they are small strokes or blips written above or below the consonants; their name is He·re·kaat' حَرَكات. Understanding the vowels in both languages is very necessary because vowels rule a language. Luckily, the author of this program dissected the vowels in both languages and has written books about them.

Spoken Arabic for English Speakers

8. The three long Arabic vowels: أَلِف واو ياء
In this book, the three Arabic long vowels are represented in (aa أَلِف) that sound like the "a" in "cat", the (ee ياء) that sounds like the "ee" in "meet", and the (oo واو) that sounds like the "oo" in "boot".

The 'elif: أَلِف
1. The long Arabic vowel "aa" is called 'elif أَلِف and it is normally pronounced like the "a" in "father" but changes to like the "a" in "man" when next to an "emphatic" consonant. Emphatic consonants are: (H, A, D, S, Z حُروف ألْإطْباق).
2. The 'elif meqSooreh: أَلِف مَقْصورَة is a weaker version of the 'elif sound; it sounds like the English "aw" in "law" and it occurs only at the end of Arabic words. The symbol given to it in this book is "aw" as in music: mōo'·see·qaw: موسيقى.
3. The waaw: واو
The long vowel "oo" is called waaw واو and it sounds like the "oo" in "boot". In a few words, it sounds like the long vowel ō as in bōat. The few words are mainly derived from English or other foreign languages. Examples are: raad'·yō, sti·ryō', te·li·fōon', 'ōo'·fin,'el·bōom', 'ōor·laan·dō, 'ōo'·haa·yō, dee'·trōoyt, dō'·laar, bee'·yaa·nō, te·le·fiz·yōon', rōob, kaar'·tōon, shōo'·kōo·laa·taa, mōo'·see·qaw, meA·ke·rōo'·nee, bananas: mōoz موز, and plums: khōokh خوخ. It is said that the word (bananas: mōoz موز) is derived from the Persian language.
4. The yaa': ياء
The long Arabic vowel "ee" is called yaa' ياء and it is normally pronounced like the "ee" in "meet" but it stops being a vowel and it changes to the sound of "y"; when at the beginning of words or syllables, as in Japan: yaa·baan يابان.

9. The three short Arabic vowels: فَتْحَة ضَمَة كَسْرَة
The three Arabic short vowels are represented in (e فَتْحَة) that sounds like the short English "e" in "set", (i كَسْرَة) that sounds like the short English "i" in "sit", and the (u ضَمَة) that sounds like the "u" in "put". The short Arabic vowels are not letters; instead, they are tiny blips or strokes written above or below consonants.
1. The fetHeh: فَتْحَة is represented with an "e" in this book, and it sounds like the short English vowel ĕ as in "set." When not stressed it sounds like a schwa, like the weak "e" sound in "brother". The fetHeh: فَتْحَة is not a letter but it is a blip written <u>above</u> consonants.
2. The Demeh: ضَمَة is a short vowel represented with a "u" in this book, and it sounds like the English "u" in "put". This Arabic short vowel has a strong sound, and it is also a blip written <u>above</u> consonants.
3. The kesreh: كَسْرَة is represented with an "i" in this book, and it sounds like short English vowel "i" in "sit". When stressed at the end of a word or a syllable, it sounds like the "i" in "ski." It is also a blip but it is the only vowel written <u>below</u> the consonants.

➢There is much more to learn in the Introduction and within each lesson in this book.

You need this book to learn the Arabic alphabet:
The Arabic Alphabet for English Speakers by Camilia Sadik ألْحُروف ألْأبْجَدِيَة لِمُتَكَلِّمي ألْإنْكِليزِيَة
This book caters to the specific needs of English speakers. Because of the precise transliteration, students begin to read Arabic instantly and from the first day of class. The book contains 800+ cognates. The vowels, consonants, and nine Arabic symbols are dissected. Essential rules that govern the structure of the Arabic alphabet are discovered. It is a class-tested approach, for all ages, and it works with or without a teacher. No other methodology has 40+ original features and learning techniques in one program. As a result, students learn the 28 Arabic letters and the nine symbols within a few months (one semester) and sometimes within weeks.

Lesson 1 — Pointing at a Singular Masculine Object: this هَذا

❶ **Learning Step One:** Read aloud to memorize each word's sound and meaning. If you are in a classroom, the entire class needs to read aloud together. Not reading aloud may help you understand these words, but it will not help you memorize them. No forced memorization is needed when you read aloud. After reading the words, students need to quickly break into groups of two and take a few minutes to quiz each other until words are completely memorized. The "dh" sounds like "th" in "bath":

this/ this is (masculine):	haa·dhaa	هَذا
taxi:	tek·see′	تَكْسي
door:	baab	باب
home:	beyt	بَيت
market:	sooq	سوق
book:	kitaab′	كِتاب
chair:	kur·see′	كُرْسي
window:	shu·baak′	شُباك
ka·bob	ke′·baab	كَباب
tea	shaa′·y	شاي

➢ Arabic does not use the articles "a" or "an" before a noun. In Arabic, "a radio" would be "radio" (raad·yōo راديو). The "this" in Arabic means "this is" without the "is." For example, "This is a radio." would be (this radio: haa·dhaa raad·yōo هَذا راديو).

➢ See the Introduction in this book to learn the details about the Arabic long and short vowels.

❷ **Learning Step Two:** Read aloud to learn the sentence pattern (this is + an object):
See how you can make unlimited number of sentences, as in (this is + an object):

haa·dhaa tek·see′. haa·dhaa baab. haa·dhaa beyt. haa·dhaa sooq. haa·dhaa kitaab. haa·dhaa kur·see′. haa·dhaa shu·baak′. haa·dhaa ke′·baab. haa·dhaa shaa′·y.

هَذا تَكْسي. هَذا باب. هَذا بَيت. هَذا سوق. هَذا كِتاب. هَذا كُرْسي. هَذا شُباك. هَذا كَباب. هَذا شاي.

❸ **Learning Step Three:** Close your books and speak aloud with the pattern you learned above, as in (this is a house هَذا بَيت) plus all other old sentence patterns that you learned during previous lessons. Since this is only the first lesson, you may use only one pattern.

❹ **Learning Step Four:** Using the above pattern, write as many sentences as you can remember.

Learn these extra easy words; they are cognates. You may add these words to your Arabic vocabulary and begin to use them in old and new sentence patterns like (this is a radio: haa·dhaa raad·yōo هَذا رادْيو):

radio: raad′·yōo	رادْيو
stereo: sti·ryōo′	سْتيرْيو
piano: bee·yaa′·nōo	بيانو
television: te·le·fiz·yōon′	تَلَفِزْيون
telephone: te·li·fōon′	تَلَفون
air conditioner: 'eyr·kin′·di·shin	أيرْكِنْدِشِن
microwave: maay′·krōo·weyf	مايْكرو وَيف
oven: 'ōo′·fin	أُوفِن
bus: baaS	باص
plug: blek	بْلَك
garage: ke·raaj′	كَراج
file: faa′·yel	فايَل
album: 'el·bōom′	أَلْبوم
shampoo: shaam′·boo	شامْبو
powder: baaw′·dir	باوْدِر
dollar: dōo′·laar	دولار
thermos: thir′·mus	ثِرْمُس
film: film	فِلم
taxi: tek·see′	تَكْسي
boot: boot	بوت
gas: ghaaz	غاز
cotton: quTn	قُطْن
blouse: blooz	بْلوز
robe: rōob	روب
blanket: blaan′·keyt	بْلانْكَيِت

bicycle: baay′·si·kil بايْسِكِل

vitamin: fee′·taa·meen فيتامين

office: 'ōo′·fees أوفيس

grass: He·sheesh′ حَشيش

cardboard box/cartoons: kaar′·tōon كارْتون

deer/gazelle: ghe·zaal′ غَزال

bugs: beq بَق

Learn the above extra words in this sentence pattern:

haa·dhaa tek·see.′ haa·dhaa baab. haa·dhaa beyt. haa·dhaa sooq. haa·dhaa kitaab. haa·dhaa kur·see′. haa·dhaa shu·baak′. haa·dhaa ke′·baab. haa·dhaa shaa′·y. haa·dhaa raad′·yōo. haa·dhaa sti·ryōo′. haa·dhaa bee′·yaa·nōo. haa·dhaa te·le·fiz·yōon′. haa·dhaa te·li·fōon′. haa·dhaa 'eyr·kin′·di·shine haa·dhaa maay′·krōo·weyf. haa·dhaa 'ōo′·fin haa·dhaa klaaS. haa·dhaa ke·raaj′. haa·dhaa faa′·yel. haa·dhaa 'el·bōom′. haa·dhaa shaam·boo′. haa·dhaa baaw′·dir. haa·dhaa dōo′·laar. haa·dhaa thir′·mus. haa·dhaa film. haa·dhaa boot. haa·dhaa ghaaz. haa·dhaa quTn. haa·dhaa blooz. haa·dhaa ben·Te·loon′. haa·dhaa rōob. haa·dhaa blaan′·keyt. haa·dhaa baay′·si·kil. haa·dhaa fee′·taa·meen. haa·dhaa 'ōo′·fees. haa·dhaa He·sheesh′. haa·dhaa kaar′·tōon. haa·dhaa ghe·zaal′.

هَذا تَكْسي. هَذا باب. هَذا بَيت. هَذا سوق. هَذا كِتاب. هَذا كُرْسي. هَذا شُباك. هَذا كَباب. هَذا شاي. هَذا راديو. هَذا سْتيريو. هَذا بِيانو. هَذا تَلَفِزْيون. هَذا تَلَفون. هَذا أيرْكِنْدِشِن. هَذا مايْكروْوَيف. هَذا أوفِن. هَذا كُلاص. هَذا كَراج. هَذا فايَل. هَذا أَلْبوم. هَذا شامْبو. هَذا باوْدِر. هَذا دولار. هَذا ثِرمِس. هَذا فِلم. هَذا بوت. هَذا غاز. هَذا قُطن. هَذا بْلوز. هَذا تَلَفون. هَذا روب. هّذا بْلانكيت. هَذا بايْسِكِل. هَذا فيتامين. هَذا أوفيس. هَذا حَشيش. هَذا كارْتون. هَذا غَزال.

Learn these extra words and you may learn them in time as needed; especially if you need them for traveling. You may use any of these words in the same sentence pattern you just learned, as in (this is an airport: haa·dhaa me·Taar هَذا مَطار):

airport: me·Taar′   مَطار

restaurant: meT′·Aem   مَطْعَم

street: shaa′·riA   شارِع

hotel: fin′·diq   فِنْدِق

dictionary: qaa′·moos   قاموس

address: Ain·waan′   عِنْوان

post office/mail: be·reed′   بَريد

key: mif·taaH′   مِفْتاح

lock: qifl   قِفل

ceiling: seqf   سَقْف

wall: Haa′·′iT   حائِط

fence: si·yaaj′   سِياج

bathroom: Hem·maam′   حَمّام

kitchen: meT′·bekh   مَطْبَخ

stove: furn   فُرن

backgammon: Taaw′·lee   طاوْلي

chess: shiT′·rinj   شِطْرِنْج

one pair of pants: ben·Te·loon′   بَنْطَلون

swim suit: maa′·yōo   مايو

bathtub: baan′·yōo   بانْيو

museum: met′·Hef   مَتْحَِف

pen: qe′·lem   قَلَم

notebook: def′·ter   دَفْتَر

soap: Saa′·boon   صابون

The White House: ′elbeyt ′el′eb′·yeD   ألْبَيت ألأبَيض

Directions to be Followed Rigorously

1. This learning process is cumulative; do not fall behind in class. Follow the same four learning steps after every new lesson.

2. Be sure you are reading the practice lessons aloud and saying the sentences aloud. If you find yourself studying but not learning, it is because you aren't reading aloud, and you aren't following the rest of the directions given to you in this book. This memorization method works only if all the instructions given to you are followed rigorously. If you read silently you will understand, but you will not be able to speak. You cannot retain a perfect sentence unless your mouth utters it. So, if you haven't read aloud, it is not too late. Go back and read again aloud.

3. Begin by speaking aloud alone. Like a child learning to speak, know that the first step to acquiring a language is speaking it alone, not conversing with others. Conversations require speaking with complex grammar (all parts of speech) that you are not ready to use, and this is the reason behind people conversing for a few minutes and then shutting up. A child begins by uttering simple sounds alone, the sounds become words, and then (s)he converses with others using sentences. Moreover, a child converses with simple sentences for five years until he (s)he goes to school to learn to read and write, and then his sentences become more complete. If you wish to produce complex sentences, focus on the simple ones. Complex ones come as a natural result, without you knowing it and without you trying to force the process.

4. Avoid thinking about correct grammar when you speak. Focus only on getting your point across. Don't just think a sentence; say it! Don't worry if you make mistakes, you learn best from your own mistakes. Simply, follow the instructions.

5. Create your own sentences from the patterns you learned. Combine old and new sentence patterns from previous lessons and speak aloud until you achieve fluency in all the learned patterns.

6. Corrections during speech are not permitted. If you need more corrections, go back to previous steps. If anyone tries to correct you, tell them "If you can understand me, please don't correct me because correcting me will make me too conscious about grammar and that will cause me to lose confidence and fluency".

7. Speak only Arabic and don't say, "How do you say?" If you wish to produce complex sentences, focus on the simple ones. Complex ones come as a natural result without you trying to force them.

8. Free yourself from worrying about making grammatically perfect sentences; you will learn best from your own mistakes

9. Focus on "what" is being said, not on "how" things are said.

10. Be very LOUD and use this step as an opportunity to develop your fluency, confidence, and memory. Use this book as a learning step to develop the ability to obliterate hesitation, saying, "How do you say," and vacillating during speech.

11. Much more time needs to be spent on Step 4. It contributes to speaking fluency by creating your own sentences. Close your books and speak aloud with new and old sentence patterns. If any teacher tends to go over this step too fast, students may stop to ask the teachers to slow down. Focus on "what" is being said, not on "how" things are said. Be very LOUD and use this step as an opportunity to develop your fluency, confidence, and memory. Use this step to develop the ability to obliterate hesitation, saying, "How do you say," and vacillating during speech.

Chapter 2 — Bring something please! جيب

❶ **Learning Step One:** Read aloud and then memorize each word's sound and meaning:

kabob: ke·baab′	كَباب
soup: soob	سوب
fish: se′·mek	سَمَك
rice: ruzz	رُزّ
please: min feD′·lek	مِن فَضْلَك
and: we- ("we" is a prefix, as in "webaab")	وَ
the bill: 'elHi·saab′	إلْحِساب
bring (command form verb): jeeb	جيب

❷ **Learning Step Two:** Read aloud to learn the sentence pattern (bring + something + please):
➤ Now you can make your own sentences out of (bring + an object + please):

jeeb ke·baab′ min feD′·lek. jeeb soob min feD′·lek. jeeb se′·mek min feD′·lek. jeeb ruzz min feD′·lek. jeeb se′·mek weruzz min feD′·lek. jeeb se′·mek weruzz wesoob, wejeeb 'elHi·saab′ min feD′·lek

جيب كَباب مِن فَضْلَك جيب سوب مِن فَضْلَك جيب سَمَك مِن فَضْلَك جيب رُزّ مِن فَضْلَك جيب سَمَك وَرُزّ مِن فَضْلَك. جيب سَمَك وَرُزّ وَسوب، وَجيب إلْحِساب مِن فَضْلَك.

Rule to find the Stressed Syllable: قاعدة ألْتَشْديد عَلى ألْمَقْطَع
The stress is on the first long vowel in a word, as in (kabob: ke·baab′ كَباب). If there is no long vowel in a word the stress is on the first syllable, as in (fish: se′·mek سَمَك).

Follow these Four Learning Steps after every New Lesson

❶ **Learning Step One:** Read aloud to memorize each word's sound and meaning.
❷ **Learning Step Two:** Read aloud to learn the new sentence pattern.
❸ **Learning Step Three:** Speak with new and old sentence patterns.
❹ **Learning Step Four:** Write as many sentences as you can remember.

➤ **Note about remembering:** If you cannot remember at least five sentences, go back, and study the above lessons again. Make sure you are reading and speaking ALOUD or you will not remember what you learned. Reading silently will help you understand what you learn but will not help you remember to use what you understood in speech. Unlike most other disciplines, a language must be SPOKEN and not merely understood. Make sure not to fall behind in your studying because this learning process is cumulative.

These are extra words to add to your vocabulary; you may use them in sentence patterns, as in (Bring hamburger please: (jeeb hem·ber·ker min feD·lek جيب هَمبَركَر من فَضْلَك):

hamburger: hem'·ber·ker	هَمبَرْكَر
ketchup: kej'··'eb	كَجَ أَب
macaroni: meA·ke·rōo'·nee	مَعْكَروني
spaghetti: sbe·key·ree'	سْبَكيري
Pepsi: bib·see'	بِبسي
7-up: se'··fin 'eb	سَفِن أَب
falafel: fe·laa'··fil	فَلافِل
garbanzo beans: Hu'·muS	حُمُص
cake/pastry: keyk	كَيك
lemons: ley'·moon'	لَيْمون
jell-O: je·lee'	جَلي
potato chips: jibs	جِبس
spinach: se·baa'··nikh	سَبانِخ
te·boo'··lee	تَبولي
gyro: shaa'·wir·maa	شاوِرْما
sugar: suk'·ker	سُكَر
curry powder: kaa'··ree	كاري
steak: steyk	سْتَيِك
sesame: sim'··sim	سِمْسِم
tahini: Te·Hee'··nee	طَحيني
pudding/custard: kaas'·ter	كاسْتَر
candy/chocolate: shōo'·koo·laa·taa	شوكولاتَا
cookie: bis·kweet'	بِسْكْويت
croissant: kre'··sent	كُرَسَنت
alcohol: ki·Hool'	كِحول

wine: ne·beedh'	نَبيذ
whiskey: wis·kee'	ويسْكي
bread: khubz	خُبْز
cheese: jibn	جِبْن
fava-beans: fool	فول
chicken: di·jaaj'	دِجاج
chicken curry: di·jaaj' kaa'·ree	دِجاج كاري
food: 'ekl	أَكْل
American food: 'ekl 'em·ree'·kee	أَكْل أَمْريكي
Arabian food: 'ekl Ae·re·bee'	أَكْل عَرَبي
Indian food: 'ekl hin·dee'	أَكْل هِنْدي
eggs: beyD	بَيض
salt: milH	مِلح
pepper: fil'·fil	فِلفِل
mustard: kher'·del	خَرْدَل
garlic: thoom	ثوم
onions: be'·Sel	بَصَل
meat: leHm	لَحم
lamb: leHm ghe'·nem	لَحم غَنَم
spice: be·haar'	بَهار
kuskus: kus'·kus/bur'·ghul	كُسْكُس/بُرْغُل
water: mey	مَي
milk: He·leeb'	حَليب
ice/snow: thelj	ثَلج
juice: Ae·Seer'	عَصير
lemon juice: Ae·Seer' ley·moon'	عَصير لَيْمون

Read aloud for extra practice:

- jeeb 'ekl 'em·ree'·kee min feD'·lek. jeeb steyk wedi·jaaj' wesoob. jeeb hem'·ber·ker wekej''·'eb wekher'·del wejeeb 'elmilH wi· 'elfil'·fil min feD'·lek, wejeeb khubz 'em·ree'·kee min feD'·lek. jeeb meA·ke·rōo'·nee wesbe·key·ree'. jeeb bib·see'. jeeb se'·fin 'eb. jeeb He·leeb'. wejeeb mey wethelj min feD'·lek.

- jeeb 'ekl Ae·re·bee' min feD'·lek. jeeb ke·baab' weshaa'·wir·maa. jeeb te·boo'·lee weley·moon' min feD'·lek. jeeb Hu'·muS, jeeb fe·laa'·fil weTe·Hee'·nee. jeeb leHm ghe'·nem wese·baa'·nikh. jeeb fool. jeeb kus'·kus. jeeb bur'·ghul. jeeb se'·mek weruzz. jeeb Ae·Seer' ley·moon', wejeeb khubz Ae·re·bee' min feD'·lek.

- jeeb 'ekl hin·dee' min feD'·lek. jeeb di·jaaj' kaa'·ree weruzz. jeeb be·haar' wethoom webe'·Sel min feD'·lek.

- jeeb beyD. jeeb jibn wekre'·sent wene'·beedh min feD'·lek.

- jeeb keyk weje·lee' wejibs wekaas'·ter weshōo'·koo·laa·taa webis·kweet'. wejeeb suk'·ker, wejeeb 'elHi·saab' min feD'·lek.

- جيب أَكْل أَمْريكي مِن فَضْلَك. جيب سْتَيك وَدِجاج وسوب. جيب هَمْبَرْكِر وكَج أَب وخَرْدَل، وجيب اَلْملح واَلْفِلْفِل مِن فَضْلَك. جيب خُبْز أَمْريكي مِن فَضْلَك. جيب مَعْكَروني وسْبَكيري. جيب بِبْسي. جيب سَفِن أَب. جيب حَليب. وجيب مَي وثَلْج مِن فَضْلَك.

- جيب أَكْل عَرَبي مِن فَضْلَك. جيب كَباب وشاورْما. جيب تَبولي وليْمون مِن فَضْلَك. جيب حُمُص، جيب فَلافِل وطَحيني. جيب لَحم غَنَم وسَبانِخ. جيب فول. جيب كُسْكُس. جيب بُرْغُل. جيب سَمَك ورُزّ, جيب عَصير لَيْمون، وجيب خُبْز عَرَبي مِن فَضْلَك.

- جيب أَكْل هِنْدي مِن فَضْلَك. جيب دِجاج كاري ورُزّ. وجيب بَهار وثوم وبَصَل مِن فَضْلَك.

- جيب بَيض. جيب جِبن وكُروسانْت ونَبيذ مِن فَضْلَك.

- جيب كَيك وجَلي وكاسْتَر وشوكولاتا وبِسْكويت وجيب سُكَّر، وجيب إِلْحِساب مِن فَضْلَك.

Spoken Arabic for English Speakers

The prefix "the": اَلـ
The *aa*'el اَلـ means "the" and it is a prefix in Arabic, as in (the door: 'elbaab اَلْبَاب). Being a prefix means it attaches to the word that follows it. The *aa*'el اَلـ can mean "the" and it can simply be a part of a person's surname or a part of a country's name. Some countries' names begin with *aa*'el (Algeria: اَلْجَزَائِر), some can't take an *aa*'el (Palestine: فَلَسْطِين), and others may take an *aa*'el اَلـ only to mean "the" (The Gulf: اَلْخَلِيج). The 'elif أ in *aa*'el اَلـ is silent because the hemzeh هَمْزَة riding on it suppresses its sound.

Sun Letters: اَلْحِروف اَلشَمْسِيَة
Fifteen of the Arabic letters are called sun letters, and they are:
سين، شين، صاد، راء، تاء، طاء، لام، جيم، نون، دال، ذال، ثاء، زاي، ضاد، ظاء.

t ت	r ر	S ص	sh ش	s س
d د	n ن	j ج	l ل	T ط
Z ظ	D ض	z ز	th ث	dh ذ

Silent L ل: The "l" in 'el اَلـ becomes silent when followed by a sun letter, as in 'el·soob اَلسّوب, 'el·shaay اَلشّاي, 'el·Se·HeeH اَلصَّحِيح, 'el·ruzz اَلرُّزّ, 'el·tek·see اَلتَّكْسِي, 'el·Taa·lib اَلطَّالِب, 'el·le·dheed اَللَّذيذ, 'el·je·meel اَلْجَمِيل, 'el·naas اَلنَّاس, 'el·di·jaaj اَلدِّجاج, 'el·dhe·heb اَلذَّهَب, 'el·thoom اَلثُّوم, 'el·zee·braa اَلزِّيبرا, 'el·De·meh اَلضَّمَة, 'el·Zaa' اَلظَّاء. If not followed by a sun letter, the 'e in 'el is usually silent, as in 'el·baab اَلْباب and as in 'el plus any other letter that is not a Sun Letter, including the vowels ('el··ōo·fin اَلأُوفِن).

The prefix (and: we وَ) becoming (wi وِ):
(we + 'el + sun letter) sounds like (wi + 'el + sun letter) as in the (and the rice: we'elruzz وَرُزّ) sounding like (wiruzz وِرُزّ). But, (we + 'el + other than a Sun Letter) sounds like (wil) as in (we'elbaab وَلْباب) changing to (wilbaab وِلْباب).

The (this: haa·dhaa هَذا) sounding like the prefix (he هَـ)
The word (this: haadhaa هَذا) followed by ('el + sun letter) sounds like (he هَـ), as in he·soob هَسوب, he·shaay هَشاي, he·Se·boon هَصابون, he·ruzz هَرُزّ, he·tek·see هَتَكْسِي, he·Taa·lib هَطالِب, he·leHm هَلَحْم, he·jaa·keyt هَجاكيت, he·naas هَناس, he·di·jaaj هَدِجاج, he·dhe·heb هَذَهَب, he·thoom هَثوم, he·zee·braa هَزيبرا, he·De·meh هَضَمَة, he·Zaa' هَظاء. If not followed by a sun letter, haa·dhaa + 'el becomes hel, as in (hel·baab هَلْباب) and (hel··ōo·fin هَلأُوفِن).

The value of learning sentence patterns vs. fixed sentences: تعَلُّم نماذج الجُمَل غير محدود
With sentence patterns, you can say an unlimited number of sentences. With one sentence pattern, perhaps you can say hundreds of sentences. Whereas learning fixed sentences, one is limited to those few sentences only. This explains the reason people say a few fixed sentences and then stopping, and they may never speak again. Saying "hello" and "goodbye", etc. is very limited.

Why should you read and speak aloud: أهَمِيَة اَلْقِراءَة بِصَوْت عالٍ
- To hear your own mistakes and learn from them.
- To hear sound and improve your pronunciation.
- To practice alone, you don't have to have another person listening to you.
- To gain confidence and fluency in speaking, reading, and spelling.
- To have this class-tested methodology work for you.
- Because more memory comes from using more senses, as in hearing the sounds.
- Because this method is different, and it doesn't work without uttering.
- Because it's not enough to think a sentence, you need to say it.
- Because speaking a language is about making sounds.

Lesson 3 Greetings: merHebaa مَرْحَبا

❶ Learning Step One: Read aloud to memorize each word's sound and meaning:

hello: mer·He·baa′	مَرْحَبا
with: me′·Ae	مَعَ
safety: se·laa′·meh	سَلامَة
goodbye: me′·Ae ′el·se·laa′·meh	مَعَ ٱلسَلامَة
yes: ′ey ′·weh	أيوَه
no: laa	لا
thanks: shuk·ren	شُكْراً
you're welcome/pardon: Aef·wen	عَفْواً
good/okay: kwey′·yes	كْوَيِّس
tea: shaay	شاي
sugar: suk′·ker	سُكَّر
without: bi′·doon	بِدون
or: ′ew	أَو
the: ′el (′el is a prefix, as in ′elbaab)	ألْـ

❷ Learning Step Two: Read aloud to learn these sentence patterns:

mer·He·baa′	مَرْحَبا
bi·bsee′?	بِبْسي؟
laa shuk′·ren	لا، شُكْراً.
shaay?	شاي؟
′ey ′·weh min feD′·lek	أيوَه مِن فَضْلَك.
shaay bi·doon′ suk′·ker?	شاي بِدون سُكَّر؟
kwey′·yes	كْوَيِّس.
shaay ′ew bi·bsee′?	شاي أو بِبْسي؟
shaay, shaay	شاي، شاي.
suk·ker?	سُكَّر؟
laa, laa bi·doon′ ′el·suk·ker	لا، لا بِدون ٱلسُكَّر.

shuk'·ren	شُكْراً.
Aef'·wen	عَفْواً.
me'·Ae 'el·se·laa'·meh	مَعَ ألسَلامَة.
haa'·dhaa be*y*t.	هَذا بَيت.
jeeb shaay min feD'·lek!	جيب شاي مِن فَضْلَك.
se'·mek w*a*ruzz min feD'·lek!	جيب سَمَك ورُزّ مِن فَضْلَك.
shaay 'ew bi·bsee'?	شاي أو بِبْسي؟
shaay bi·doon' su*k*'·ker.	شاي بِدون سُكَّر.
shaay me'·Ae su*k*'·ker?	شاي مَعَ سُكَّر؟
laa, shuk'·ren.	لا شُكْراً.

❸ **Learning Step Three:** Close your book to speak aloud with new and old sentence patterns.
❹ **Learning Step Four:** Combine old and new sentence patterns and say as many sentences as you can.

Meaning of a Schwa: معنى أَلْشوا
A schwa is a name given to any sound of a weak English vowel that is barely heard, like the "a" in beggar. Standard English dictionaries use an upside-down "e" symbol to represent the schwa sound. Arabic also has some weak sounds of vowels that fall in a syllable that is not stressed, like the final "e" in (fish: semek سَمَك). It is usually the Arabic "e" فَتْحَة and "i" كَسْرَة that can sound like a schwa. The Arabic schwa is most likely represented by an "i" كَسْرَة in Egyptian dialect, as in (black: 'eswid أَسْود) and by an "e" فَتْحَة in the Gulf area's dialect (black: 'eswed أَسْوَد).

Lesson 4 — There exists: fee في

❶ **Learning Step One:** Read aloud to memorize these words:

there exist/s: fee	في
there exist/s not: maa' fee	ما في
but: laa'·kin	لَكِن
a lot/very: ketheer	كثير
a little bit/some: shwe'·yeh	شْوَيَه
a little bit of: shwe'·yet	شْوَيَة
always: daa'·'i·men	دائِماً

❷ **Learning Step Two:** Read aloud to learn to speak with these simple sentence patterns:

fee ke·baab?	في كَباب؟
'ey·weh fee	أيْوَه في.
fee bi·bsee?	في بِبسي؟
laa maa fee	لا ما في.
fee se·mek?	في سَمَك؟
laa maa fee se·mek, laa·kin fee soob.	لا ما في سَمَك، لَكِن في سوب.
fee ruzz?	في رُزّ؟
'ey·weh fee ruzz ketheer.	أيوَه في رُزّ كْثير.
fee katheer soob 'ew shwe·yeh?	في كثير سوب أو شْوَيَه؟
fee, fee 'el·soob ketheer ketheer.	في، في، إلسوب كثير كثير.
kwey yes, jeeb shwe·yet soob.	كْوَيِّس، جيب شْوَيَة سوب.
daa·'i·men fee soob weruzz, daa·'i·men.	دائِماً في سوب ورُزّ، دائِماً.

➤ The feminine suffix (eh ـه) or (et ـة) أَلْتاء أَلْمَربوطَة
The vast majority of countries and cities' names are expressed in a feminine gender. Most of which end in the suffix (et ـة) that sounds like (eh ـه) as in Syria: sooryet سورْيَة sounding like Syria: sooryeh سورْيَه. The Arabic words for "country" is (dewleh دَوْلَة) and city is (medeeneh مَدينَة) and both end with (et ـة) that sounds like (eh ـه) and they are in a feminine form. Think of a country's name being feminine as mother earth. The suffix is pronounced as (eh ـه) or (et ـة) depending on the word that follows it. When it's followed by an owner, it is pronounced like "et" as in the owner of a (car: siy·yaa·reh) becomes (siy·yaa·ret Sam).

❸ **Learning Step Three:** Speak aloud with new and old sentence patterns.
❹ **Learning Step Four:** Write as many sentences as you can remember.

Lesson 5   Not: mish مِش

❶ Learning Step One: Read aloud to memorize each word's sound and meaning:

not: mish	مِش
most likely: Het′·men	حَتْماً
right/correct/true: Se·HeeH′	صَحيح
of course: Teb′·Aen	طَبْعاً
also/more: ke·maan′	كَمان
only/enough/but: bes	بَس
take/grab: haak (command form only)	هاك

❷ Learning Step Two: Read aloud to learn to speak with these sentence patterns:

fee shaay?	في شاي؟
Het·men fee	حَتْماً في.
Se·HeeH fee?	صَحيح في؟
Teb·Aen, fee shaay wefee keyk ke·maan.	طَبْعاً في شاي وفي كيك كَمان.
bes (but) Het·men maa fee su*k*·ker.	بَس حَتْماً ما في سُكَّر.
laa, fee, fee su*k*·ker.	لا، في، في سُكَّر.
jeeb shwe·ye*t* su*k*·ker.	جيب شْوَيَة سُكَّر.
haa·dhe su*k*·ker haak.	هاك سُكَّر هاك.
bes (only) shwe·yeh, mish k*e*theer.	بَس شْوَيَه، مِش كْثير.
haak, haak.	هاك، هاك.
bes, bes (enough) su*k*·ker, bes.	بس، بس سُكَّر ، بسْ.

❸ Learning Step Three: Speak aloud with new and old sentence patterns.

❹ Learning Step Four: Write as many sentences as you can remember.

Spoken Arabic for English Speakers

➢ The tenween تَنْوين as in شُكْراً:

The ten·ween' تَنْوين is an ending (suffix) that can have three different sounds. The first sound is like the "en" as in "taken" and in the Arabic word (thank you: shuk·ren شُكْراً). The other two sounds are "un" that sounds like the "un" in (a book: ki·taa·bun كِتابٌ) and the "in" sound as in (ki·taa·bin كِتابٍ). The "un" and "in" endings involve the grammatical structure of sentences, not just words. It is best to study them in advanced levels of Arabic in the future. In this book, we are mainly concerned with the grammar inside the words and in simple sentences. Hence, "en" ending as in shuk·ren شُكْراً is the only one we will be studying here. When first hearing the "en" sound as in شُكْراً, one assumes that it is spelled with an "n ن." However, there is no "n ن" in these tenween endings. Instead, there is a double blip sitting above the 'elif as in shuk·ren شُكْراً or above the end isolated hemzeh like this ءً as in (please: ri·jaa'·'en رِجاءً). Notice that most of these words are adverbs. Learn the tenween in these words:

thanks/thank you:	shuk'·r*aa*en	شُكْراً
you're welcome:	Aef·w*aa*en	عَفْواً
very:	ji·d*aa*en	جِداً
please (not v.):	ri·jaa'··'en	رِجاءً
a lot:	ke·thee·r*aa*en	كَثيراً
in the morning:	Se·baa·H*aa*en	صَباحاً
always:	daa·'i·m*aa*en	دائِماً
in the evening:	me·saa·*aa*'en	مَساءً
nighttime:	ley·l*aa*en	لَيْلاً
a little:	qe·lee·l*aa*en	قَليلاً
first of all:	'ew·we·l*aa*en	أَوَلاً

Lesson 6	Verbs in command form: الأفعال بصيغة الأمر

Spoken Arabic for English Speakers

❶ Learning Step One: Read aloud to memorize each word's sound and meaning:
> Verbs throughout this book are first introduced in a command form.

eat: kul   كُل

drink: 'ish·'·reb   إِشْرَب

make: sew·wee'   سَوّي

cook: 'iT·'·bukh   إِطْبُخ

buy: 'ish·ti·ree'   إِشْتَرِي

let's/ come on: yel'·leh   يَلَّه

money: floos   فْلوس

and then: webeA·deyn'   وبَعْدين

❷ Learning Step Two: Read aloud to learn to speak with these sentence patterns:

yel·leh 'ish·ti·ree se·mek weruzz. haak shwe·yet floos, we'ish·ti·ree keyk ke·maan. webeA·deyn, 'iT·bukh 'el·se·mek wi·ruzz wekul. webeA·deyn, sew·wee shwe·yet shaay we'ish·reb 'ilshaay wekul 'lkeyk.

يَلَّه إِشْتَرِي سَمَك ورُزّ. هاك شْوَيَة فْلوس، وإِشْتِرِي كَيك كَمان. وبَعْدَين إِطْبُخ أَلسَمَك وأَلْرُزّ وكُل. وبَعْدَين، سَوّي شْوَيَة شاي وإِشْرَب أَلْشاي وكُل أَلْكَيك.

❸ Learning Step Three: Speak aloud with new and old sentence patterns.

❹ Learning Step Four: Write as many sentences as you can remember.

Lesson 7 — Adjectives: ألصِفات

❶ Learning Step One: Read aloud to memorize each word's sound and meaning:

big/large/old in age: kebeer   كَبير
jacket/blazer: jaa'·keyt   جاكيت
black: 'es '·wed   أَسْوَد
beautiful: je·meel'   جَميل
excellent: mum·taaz'   مُمْتاز
delicious: le·dheedh'   لَذيذ

❷ Learning Step Two: Read aloud to learn to speak with these patterns:

◆ 'eljaa·keyt 'es·wed. 'eljaa·keyt je·meel. 'eljaa·keyt mish kebeer ketheer. 'eljaa·keyt 'es·wed weje·meel wemish kebeer ketheer. Teb·Aen, 'el'es·wed daa·'i·men je·meel, daa·'i·men.
◆ hel·kitaab mum·taaz; haak floos we'ish·ti·ree hel·kitaab.
◆ hel·se·mek le·dheedh ketheer; kul hel·se·mek 'el·le·dheedh kul.
◆ Het·men hel·sooq kebeer ketheer, mish Se·HeeH?
◆ laa, hel·sooq kebeer, laa·kin mish kebeer ketheer. fee sooq kebeer wefee sooq mish kebeer ketheer.
◆ haak hel·jaa·keyt 'elkwey·yes, haak.

◆ إِلْجاكيت أَسْوَد. إِلْجاكيت جَميل. إِلْجاكيت مِش كَبير كَثير. إِلْجاكيت أَسْوَد وجَميل ومِش كَبير كَثير. طَبعاً ألأَسْوَد دائماً جَميل، دائماً. ◆ هَلْكِتاب مُمْتاز. هاك فُلوس وإِشْتري هَلْكِتاب.
◆ هَلْسَمَك لَذيذ كَثير؛ كُل هَاسَمَك إِلْلَذيذ كُل. ◆ حَتْماً هالْسوق كَبير كَثير، مِش صَحيح؟ ◆ لا، هالْسوق كَبير لَكِن مِش كَبير كَثير. في سوق كَبير وفي سوق مِش كَبير كَثير. ◆ هاك هَلْجاكيت ألْكُوَّيس، هاك.

In Arabic, nouns precede adjectives: الأَسِم قَبل الصِفة
"a good rice" is expressed "rice good" (ruzz kweyyis رُزّ كوَيِّس). Similarly, "a white house" is expressed (house white: beyt 'ebyeD بَيْت أَبيَض). In Arabic, there is no "is" and "big door" can be expressed:
- the door is big / the door big: 'elbaab kebeer ألْباب كَبير
- the door is big / the door it is big: 'elbaab huwe kebeer ألْباب هو كَبير
- the <u>specific</u> door that is big / the door the big: 'elbaab 'elkebeer ألْباب ألْكَبير
- <u>any door</u> a door is big / door big: باب كَبير

Learn these extra words and you may use them in the same sentence patterns you just learned, as in (this house is beautiful: helbeyt jemeel هالْبَيت جَميل). These adjectives are in a singular masculine form. Remember that nouns precede adjectives in Arabic (house beautiful بَيت جَميل) and there is no "is" in Arabic:

beautiful: je·meel' جَميل
tall: Te·weel' طَويل
small/young in age: Se·gheer' صَغير
short: qe·Seer' قَصير
sad: He·zeen' حَزين
fat: Se·meen' سَمين
thick: thkheen ثَخين
clean: ne·Zeef' نَظيف
kind/soft: le·Teef' لَطيف
skinny: Ne·Heef' نَحيف
weak: Ze·Aeef' ضَعيف
humorous: Te·reef' طَريف
light weighted: khe·feef' خَفيف
great: Ae·Zeem' عَظيم
wise: He·keem' حَكيم
in good health: se·leem' سَليم
generous: ke·reem' كَريم
old/ancient: qe·deem' قَديم
wide: Ae·reeD' عَريض
new: je·deed' جَديد
far: be·Aeed' بَعيد
happy: se·Aeed' سَعيد
fast: se·reeA' سَريع
deep: Ae·meeq' عَميق

simple: be·seeT'	بَسيط
difficult: SeAb	صَعْب
smart: dhe·kee'	ذَكي
natural: Te·bee'·Aee	طَبيعي
conscious: waa'·Aee	واعي
high: Aaa'·lee	عالي
expensive: ghaa'·lee	غالي
hollow/ empty: khaa'·lee	خالي
sweet/good looking: Hi·loo'	حِلو
happy: fer·Haan'	فَرْحان
mad: zeA·laan'	زَعْلان
tired: teA·baan'	تَعْبان
artist: fen·naan'	فَنّان
humanist: 'in·saa'·nee	إنْساني
educated: daa'·ris	دارِس
intellectual: mu'·the·qef	مُثَقَف
well-read: qaa'·ri' jey·id	قارِيء جَيْد
low: waa'·Ti'	واطِيء
honest: Saa'·diq	صادِق
narrow/tight: Zey'·yiq	ضَيِّق
joyful: mum'·tiA	مُمْتِع
lovely: meH'·boob	مَحْبوب
slow: be·Tee''	بَطيء
round: mdew'·wer	مْدَوَّر
strong/powerful: qe·wee'	قَوي
giant: Aim·laaq'	عِمْلاق

gigantic: Haa'··'il هائِل
illiterate: 'u·mee' أُمي
literate: mish 'u·mee' مِش أُمي
ignorant: jaa'·hil جاهِل

The colors: *'el*··'el·waan' اَلألْوان
black: 'es '··wed أَسْوَد
blue: 'ez '··req أَزْرَق
light blue: 'ez '··req baa'·hit أَزْرَق باهِت
dark blue: 'ez '··req gh'aa'·miq أَزْرَق غامِق
red: 'eH '··mer أَحْمَر
pink: wer·dee' وَرْدي
green: 'ekh '··Der أَخْضَر
khaki: khaa'·kee خاكي
purple: be·nef·se·jee' بَنَفْسَجي
lilac: be·nef·se·jee' baa'·hit بَنَفْسَجي باهِت
brown: bu·nee' بُني
beige: bu·nee' baa'·hit بُني باهِت
gold: dhe·he·bee' ذَهَبي
silver: fu·Dee' فُضي
yellow: 'eS '··fer أَصْفَر
orange: bur·te·qaa'·lee بُرْتَقالي
blond: 'esh '··qer أَشْقَر
gray: ri·Saa'·See رِصاصي
white: 'eb'··yed أَبْيَض
gray hair: white hair شَعْر أَبْيَض

Do Learning Steps ❸ and ❹

Lesson 8 — Adverbs: ألظُروف

❶ Learning Step One: Read aloud to memorize each word's sound and meaning:

by the means of/in: bi (bi is a prefix)	بِـ
in a hurry: b*i*sur'·Aeh	بِسُرْعَة
in English: bi''*e*l·'in·ke·lee'·zee	بِألإنْكِليزي
in Arabic: bi''*e*l·Ae·re·bee'	بِألْعَرَبي
study: 'ud'·rus	أُدْرُس
speak: 'it'·kel·lim	إتْكَلِّم
first/first of all: '*e*·we·laan'	أوَلاً
means: yeA·nee'	يَعْني
see: shoof	شوف

❷ Learning Step Two: Read aloud to learn to speak with these sentence patterns:

♦ 'ud·rus bi '*e*l·'in·ke·lee·zee w*e*'it·kel·lim bi '*e*l·Ae·re·bee b*i*sur·Aeh

♦ shoof hel·k*i*taab haa·dha '*e*·we·laan, 'ud·rus '*e*l·Ae·re·bee bi '*e*l·'in·ke·lee·zee, webeA·deyn 'ud·rus bes bi '*e*l·Ae·re·bee.

♦ haa·dhaa yeA·nee: '*e*·we·laan, 'ud·rus bi '*e*l·'in·ke·lee·zee, webeA·deyn 'ud·rus bi '*e*l·Ae·re·bee.

♦ أُدْرُس بِألإنْكِليزي وإتْكَلِّم بِألْعَرَبي بِسُرْعَة. ♦ شوف هَلْكِتاب هذا أوَلاً، أُدْرُس ألْعَرَبي بِألإنْكِليزي، وبعدين أُدْرُس بِألْعَرَبي. ♦ هِذا يَعْني: أوَلاً، أُدْرُس بِألإنْكِليزي، وبعدين أُدْرُس بِألْعَرَبي.

❸ Learning Step Three: Speak aloud with new and old sentence patterns.
❹ Learning Step Four: Write as many sentences as you can remember.

Verbs precede adverbs: ألْفِعل يَسْبِق ألظَرف
Just like English, verbs come before adverbs in Arabic:
(Sam drives quickly: Sam y*e*sooq bisurAeh بِسُرْعَة سام يسوق).
It makes sense to have the verbs first because adverbs describe these verbs, and without verbs there cannot be adverbs.

Lesson 9   Places: ألأماكن

❶ Learning Step One: Read aloud to memorize each word's sound and meaning:

where: weyn   وين

place: me·kaan'   مَكان

close/near: qe·reeb'   قَريب

close to (expressed as near from): qe·reeb' min   قَريب مِن

go: rooH   روح

come: te·Aaal' (only in command form, doesn't conjugate)   تَعال

bus: baaS   باص

here: hi·naa'   هِنا

there: hi·naak'   هِناك

from: min   مِن

from the (min +'el = mnil or mni): mnil   مْنِلـ

to: li (li is a prefix)   لِـ

to the: lil (lil is a prefix)   لِلـ

bank: benk   بَنك

❷ Learning Step Two: Read aloud to learn to speak with these sentence patterns:
Questions in Arabic are asked by changing the voice to a question tone (intonation), with no change in the word order. When writing, simply add a question mark.

◆ weyn 'elbeyt?
◆ 'elbeyt hi·naa qe·reeb min hel·me·kaan.
◆ weyn 'el·sooq?
◆ 'el·sooq hi·naak mish qe·reeb min hi·naa.
◆ 'elbenk qe·reeb min hi·naa?
◆ laa, 'elbenk ke·maan mish qe·reeb.
◆ 'elbenk qe·reeb mnil·sooq?
◆ 'ey·weh Teb·Aen, Het·men fee benk qe·reeb mnil·sooq. laa·kin haa·dha laa yeA·nee 'i·ne·hu (that) 'elbank qe·reeb min hi·naa.
◆ kwey·yes, kwey·yes, rooH lil·benk 'e·we·len, wejeeb 'elfloos mnil·benk. webeA·deyn, rooH li*l*·sooq we'ish·ti·ree jaa·keyt

mni*l*·sooq. w*e*min hi·naak te·Aaal hi·naa 'ew rooH li*l*·bey*t* re'·sen (directly). kwey·yes 'ew laa?

♦ laa Tab·Aen haa·dha mish kwey·yes, li·'e·ne·hu (because) maa fee baaS mni*l*·sooq li*l*·bey*t*.

♦ Se·HeeH, Se·HeeH Het·men maa fee baaS mnie*l*·sooq li*l*·bey*t*. kwey·yes rooH bi'*el*·tek·see. 'ey·weh Se·HeeH, maa fee baaS, bes daa·'i·man fee tek·see.

♦ Teb·Aen, Het·men daa·'i·men fee tek·see daa·'i·men.

♦ وَين أَلْبَيت؟

♦ أَلْبَيت هِنا قريب مِن هَلمَكان.

♦ وَين أَلْسوق؟

♦ أَلْسوق هِناك مِش قَريب مِن هِنا.

♦ إِلْبَنْك قَريب مِن هِنا؟

♦ لا، إِلْبَنْك كَمان مِش قَريب.

♦ إِلْبَنْك قَريب مْنِل سوق؟

♦ أَيْوَه طَبْعاً، حَتْماً في بَنْك قَريب مِنِلْسوق. لَكِن هَذا لا يَعْني أَنَهُ إِلْبَنْك قَريب مِن هِنا.

♦ كُوَّيِّس، كُوَّيِّس، روح لِلْبَنْك أَوَّلاً وجيب الْفِلوس مِنِلْبَنْك. وبَعْدين روح لِلسوق وإِشْتِري جاكيت مِنِلْسوق. ومِن هِناك تَعال هِنا أَو روح لِلْبَيت رَأساً. كُوَّيِّس أو لا؟

♦ لا طَبْعاً، هَذا مِش كُوَّيِّس لِأَنَهُ ما في باص مِن إِلْسوق لِلْبَيت.

♦ صَحيح، صَحيح، حَتْماً ما في باص مِنِلْسوق لِلْبَيت. كُوَّيِّس روح بِلْتَكْسي. أَيْوَه صَحيح ما في باص، بَس دائِماً في تَكْسي.

♦ طَبْعاً، حَتْماً دائِماً في تَكْسي دائِماً.

Some Arabic prefixes: بَعض أَلْبادِئآت في أَلْعَرَبِيَة
It saves space on a page to have a large number of prefixes in Arabic. Here are a few examples:
and: we-: وَ: (sugar: wesukker وَسُكَّر)
the: 'el-: أَلْ: (the book: 'elkitaab أَلْكِتاب)
to: li-: لِ: (to Baghdad: **li**beghdaad لِبَغْداد)
to the: lil- لِلْ: (lilsooq لِلْسوق)
These are in spoken, not formal Arabic:
from the: min + 'el = mnil- مْنِل: (from the market: mnilsooq مْنِل سوق)
this: hel- هَل: (this book: helkitaab هَلْكِتاب)

Do Learning Steps ❸ and ❹.

Lesson 10 Traveling: ألسَّفَر

❶ Learning Step One: Read aloud to memorize each word's sound and meaning:

travel: saa'·fir	سافِر
visit: zoor	زور
take: khudh	خُذ
airport: me·Taar'	مَطار
now: 'elaan	ألآن
because: li'e'·ne·hu	لِأَنَهُ
for an example: me·the·len'	مَثَلاً
river: nehr	نَهر
The Nile River: nehr 'el·neel'	نَهر إلنيل
museum: met'·Hef	مَتْحَف
theater: mes'·reH	مَسْرَح
film: film	فِلم
The Middle East: 'el·sherq 'elaw'·seT	ألشَرْق ألأَوْسَط

❷ Learning Step Two: Read aloud to learn to speak with these sentence patterns:

zoor 'el·sherq 'elew·seT li'e·ne·hu 'el·sherq 'elew·seT me·kaan kwey·yes weje·meel ketheer ketheer. me·the·len, rooH shoof nehr 'el·neel. wemin hi·naak, khudh tek·see 'ew baaS werooH zoor 'el·met·Hef, 'ew rooH lil·mes·reH, 'ew rooH lil·sooq 'elkebeer, 'ew rooH shoof film Ae·re·bee. yel·leh rooH lil·me·Taar 'elaan wesaa·fir lil·'el·sherq 'elaw·seT.

زور ألشَرْق ألأَوْسَط، لِأَنَهُ ألشَرْق ألأَوْسَط مَكان كوَّيِس وجَميل كَثير كَثير. مَثَلاً، روح شوف نَهر ألنيل. ومِن هناك، خُذ تَكْسي أو باص وروح زور ألمَتْحَف، أو روح لِلمَسْرَح، أو روح لِلسوق ألكَبير، أو روح شوف فِلم عَرَبي. يَلَه روح لِلمَطار وسافِر لِلشَرْق ألأَوْسَط.

❸ Learning Step Three: Speak aloud with new and old sentence patterns.
❹ Learning Step Four: Write as many sentences as you can remember.

Read these extra words aloud. You may use any of these words in sentence patterns about places like the ones you just learned:

restaurant: meT'·Aem مَطْعَم

street: shaa'·riA شارِع

hotel: fin'·diq فِنْدِق

post office: be·reed' بَريد

bathroom: Hem·maam' حَمّام

kitchen: meT'·bekh مَطْبَخ

park: mun'·te·zeh مُنْتَزَه

mountain: je'·bel جَبَل

coffee shop: meq·haa' مَقْهى

store: du·kaan' دُكان

Spelling: تَهَجّي
1. When you see ('el) at the beginning of a word or syllable, it is actually spelled with a silent "aa" أَلِف before it. For instance, 'ekl is actually spelled *aa*'ekl أكل with a silent "aa" أَلِف before it. The hemzeh هَمْزَة that rides on top of the 'elif tends to suppress the sound of 'elif. Another example is 'elHisaab that is actually spelled *aa*'elHisaab with a silent 'elif before it ألحِساب.

2. When you see the word "this" that means "haadhaa", it is spelled hedhaa هَذا.

3. When you see the word "but" that means "laakin", it is spelled "lekin" لَكِن.

Grammar: قَواعِد
Questions are asked by changing the voice to a question tone (intonation), with no change in the word order. When writing, simply add a question mark.

Culture: ثُراث
Words like "thank you" and "please" are not excessively used in Arabic, especially among friends and family members. If one continues to use them, friends, and family members me say, "What's wrong?" Such words are usually used in formal settings, not among friends. Friends in the Middle East don't thank each other in words but in action. Subconsciously, Arabic speakers to view excessive as an attempt to place walls among friends, and sometimes they see the person that overuse these words as a salesperson or a person who wants to get away from paying back the favor by simply saying thank you; they want to see "thank you" in deeds, not in words. Of course, not every country in the Middle East has this same exact culture. For instance, this is truer in the Gulf area and less true in Egypt, Lebanon, and Syria, wherein many survive on tourism and must use such polite words as they entertain visitors.

Do Learning Steps ❸ and ❹.

Summary of the Learned Lessons in Part One (107 Words)

Lesson 1:

this/ this is:	haa·dhaa	هَذا
taxi:	tek·see′	تَكْسي
door:	baab	باب
home:	be*y*t	بَيت
market:	sooq	سوق
book:	k*i*taab′	كِتاب
chair:	kur·see′	كُرْسي
window:	shu·baak′	شُباك
ka·bob	ke′·baab	كَباب
tea	shaa′·y	شاي

Lesson 2:

kabob:	ke·baab′	كَباب
soup:	soob	سوب
fish:	se′·mek	سَمَك
rice:	ruzz	رُزّ
please:	min feD′·lek	مِن فَضْلَك
and:	we-	وَ
the bill:	′*el*Hi·saab′	إلْحِساب
bring:	jeeb	جيب

Lesson 3:

hello:	mer·He·baa′	مَرْحَبا
with:	me′·Ae	مَع
safety:	se·laa′·meh	سَلامَة
goodbye:	me′·Ae ′e*l*·se·laa′·meh	مَع أَلسَلامَة
yes:	′ey ′·weh	أَيوَه
no:	laa	لا
thanks:	shuk·ren	شُكْراً
you're welcome:	Aef·wen	عَفْواً
good/okay:	kwe*y*′·yes	كْوَيِّس
tea:	shaay	شاي
sugar:	su*k*′·ker	سُكَّر
without:	bi′·doon	بِدون
or:	′ew	أو
the:	′el	أَلْـ

Lesson 4:

there exist/s:	fee	في
there exist/s not:	maa′ fee	ما في

but:	laa′·kin	لَكِن
a lot/very:	k*e*theer	كثير
a little bit/some:	shwe′·ye**h**	شْوَيَه
a little bit of:	shwe′·ye**t**	شْوَيَة
always:	daa′·'i·men	دائِماً

Lesson 5:

not:	mish	مِش
most likely:	H*e*t′·men	حَتْماً
right/correct/true:	S*e*·HeeH′	صَحيح
of course:	T*e*b′·Aen	طَبْعاً
also/more:	ke·maan′	كَمان
only/enough/but:	bes	بَس
take/grab:	haak	هاك

Lesson 6:

eat:	kul	كُل
drink:	′ish′·reb	إشْرَب
make:	sew·wee′	سَوِّي
cook:	′iT ′·bukh	إطْبُخ
buy:	′ish·ti·ree′	إشْتَري
let's/ come on:	yel′·leh	يَلَّه
money:	floos	فْلوس
and then:	w*e*beA·deyn′	وبَعْدين

Lesson 7:

big/large/old:	k*e*beer	كَبير
jacket/blazer:	jaa′·keyt	جاكيت
black:	′es′·wed	أَسْوَد
beautiful:	je·meel′	جَميل
excellent:	mum·taaz′	مُمْتاز
delicious:	le·dheedh′	لَذيذ

Lesson 8:

by the means of/in:	bi (bi is a prefix)	بِـ
fast/in a hurry:	b*i*sur′·Aeh	بِسُرْعَة
in English:	bi′′*e*l·′in·ke·lee′·zee	بِألإنْكِليزي
in Arabic:	bi′′*e*l·Ae·re·bee′	بِألْعَرَبي
study:	′ud′·rus	أُدْرُس
speak:	′it′·kel·lim	إتْكَلَّم
first/first of all:	′e·we·laan′	أَوَلاً
means:	yeA·nee′	يَعْني

see:	shoof	شوف

Lesson 9:

places:	place: mekaan	مَكان
where:	weyn	وَين
place:	me·kaan'	مَكان
close/near:	qe·reeb'	قَريب
close to:	qe·reeb' min	قَريب مِن
go:	rooH	روح
come:	te·Aaal'	تَعال
bus:	baaS	باص
here:	hi·naa'	هِنا
there:	hi·naak'	هِناك
from:	min	مِن
from the:	mnil	مْنِل
to:	li (li is a prefix)	لِـ
to the:	lil (lil is a prefix)	لِلـ
bank:	benk	بَنك

Lesson 10:

travel:	saa'·fir	سافِر
visit:	zoor	زور
take:	khudh	خُذ
airport:	me·Taar'	مَطار
now:	'elaan	ألآن
because:	li'e'·ne·hu	لِأَنَهُ
for an example:	me·the·len'	مَثَلاً
river:	nehr	نَهر
The Nile River:	nehr 'el·neel'	نَهر إلنيل
museum:	met'·Hef	مَتْحَف
theater:	mes'·reH	مَسْرَح
film:	film	فِلم
The Middle East:	'el·sherq 'elaw'·seT	ألْشَرق ألأَوْسَط

Place the short vowels (حَرَكات) and other Arabic symbols on the Arabic text:

- merhebaa. — مرحبا
- 'elAerebee kweyyes? — العربي كويس؟
- 'eyweh, TebAen 'elAerebee kweyyes ketheer. — ايوه، طبعا العربي كويس كثير.
- haadhaa 'elbeyt kebeer ketheer. — هذا بيت كبير كثير.
- SeHeeH helbeyt kebeer wemumtaaz kemaan. — صحيح هلبيت كبير وممتاز كمان.
- weyn fee taksee? — وين في تكسي؟
- fee texsee qereeb min hinaa. — في تكسي قريب من هنا.
- haadhaa baab 'eswed? — هذا باب اسود.
- laa, helbaab mish bes 'eswed. — لا، هالباب مش بس اسود.
- haadhaa 'elsooq mish qereeb. — هذا السوق مش قريب.
- bes fee sooq qereeb mnilbenk. — بس فس سوق قريب من البنك.
- helkitaab mumtaaz. — هالكتاب ممتاز.
- 'udrus helkitaab 'elmumtaaz. — ادرس هالكتاب الممتاز.
- helkursee qereeb ketheer mnishubaak. — هالكرسي قريب كثير من الشباك.
- kweyyes, khudh 'elkursee min hinaa. — كويس، خذ الكرسي من هنا.
- helredyoo qereeb ketheer min 'elstiryoo. — هالراديو قريب كثير من الستيريو.
- fee kemaan redyoo hinaak. — في كمان راديو هناك.
- yelleh teAaal 'udrus 'elkitaab 'elaan. — يله تعال ادرس الكتاب الآن.
- kittaab 'elAerebee 'ew kitaab 'elHisaab? — كتاب العربي او كتاب الحساب؟
- mish kitaab 'elHisaab welaa kitaab 'elAerebee. — مش كتاب الحساب ولا كتاب العربي.
- kitaab 'elinkleezee? — كتاب الانكليزي؟
- laa, laa, kitaab 'elbiyaanoo, 'elbiyaanoo. — لا، لا، كتاب البيانو، البيانو.
- weyn 'elbiyanoo 'elkebeer? — وين البيانو الكبير؟
- qereeb mniltelefizyoon. — قريب من التلفزيون.
- 'eltelefizyoon mish kweyyes. — التلفزيون مش كويس.
- mish daa'imen 'eltelefizyoon mish kweyyes. — مش دائما التلفزيون مش كويس.
- 'eyweh daa'imen 'eltelefizyoon mish kweyyes. — ايوه دائما التلفزيون مش كويس.
- heltelifoon 'eswed. — هتلفون اسود.
- laakin, haadhaa hinaa telifoon mish 'eswed. — لاكن، هذا هنا تلفون مش اسود.
- min weayn hel'oofin? — من وين هاتلفون؟
- haadhaa min 'emreekaa. — هذا من امريكا.
- laakin hel'oofen haadhaa mnilyaabaan. — لكن هلاوفن هذا من اليابان.
- wehaadhaa 'elmaaykrooweyf min hinaa. — وهذا المايكرو ويف من هنا.
- helklaaS jedeed (new) wehelthirmus jedeed kemaan. — هلكلاص جديد والثرمس جديد كمان.
- 'elkeraaj mesdood (closed). — الكراج مسدود.
- 'elfeyel 'eSfer (yellow). — الفايل اصفر.
- hel shemboo kweyyes ketheer. — هشامبو كويس كثير.
- khudh 'eldooler weshtiree kertoon Heleeb. — خذ الدولار واشتري كارتون حليب.
- haadhaa blooz qutn. — هذا بلوز قطن.
- 'elfilm kaan (was) mumtaaz. — الفلم كان ممتاز.
- rooH shoof helfilm. — روح شوف هلفلم.

- zoor 'elsherq 'el'ewseT.   زور الشرق الاوسط.
- 'elmeT Aem qereeb mnil muntezeh (park).   المطعم قريب من المنتزه.
- yelleh haak 'elkitaab werooH lilmuntezeh 'elaan.   يله هاك الكتاب وروح للمنتزه الآن.
- zoor shaariA 'elresheed bibeghdaad.   زور شارع الرشيد ببغداد.
- 'in·zil (stay in) bifindiq kweyyes.   انزل بفندق كويس.
- rooH lilbereed wejeeb 'elbereed min hinaak.   روح للبريد وجيب البريد من هناك.
- 'ewelen khudh 'elfloos webeAdeyn rooH hinaak.   اولا خذ الفلوس وبعدين روح هناك.
- 'iTbukh bilmeTbekh, yeAnee mish hinaa.   اطبخ بالمطبخ، يعني مش هنا.
- hel·mun·te·zeh qereeb mnilmeqhaw.   هلمنتزه قريب من المقهى.
- zoor 'eljebel bikelifoornyaa.   زور الجبل بكاليفورنيا.
- 'eldukaan hinaak.   الدكان هناك.
- helboot mu·reeH (comfortable).   هلبوت مريح.
- 'elquTn fee miSr (Egypt) 'ebyeD ketheer.   القطن في مصر ابيض كثير.
- 'elghaaz (the gas) ghaa·lee (expensive).   الغاز غالي.
- helbenTeloon jemeel meAe hel blooz.   هلبنطلون جميل مع هلبلوز.
- haadhaa blaankeyt mish roob.   هذا بلانكيت مش روب.
- haadhaa baaysikil se·reeA (fast)   هذا بايسكل سريع.
- haadhaa feetaameen mu·feed (useful)   هذا فيتامين مفيد.
- haadhaa 'oofees mre·teb (tidy)   هذا اوفيس مرتب.
- haadhaa Hesheesh 'ekh·Der (green)   هذا حشيش اخضر.
- haadhaa film kaartoon.   هذا فلم كارتون.
- Hetmen haadhaa ghezaal 'ef·ree·qee (African).   حتما هذا غزال افريقي.
- khudh teksee lilmeTaar li'enehu 'elmeTaar mish qereeb.   خذ تكسي للمطار لانه المطار مش قريب.
- Hetmen fee meTAem hinaak.   حتما في مطعم هناك.
- helshaa·riA Ae·reeD (wide)   هشارع عريض.
- fee findiq qereeb mnilmeTaar?   في فندق قريب من المطار.
- fee qaamoos inkleezee-Arebee feel heldukaan?   في قاموس عربي انكليزي في هدكان.
- wayn helAinwaan min feDlek?   وين هالعنوان من فضلك؟
- weyn 'elbereed?   وين البريد؟
- 'elbereed qereeb 'ew beAeed (far) min hinaa?   البريد قريب او بعيد من هنا؟
- khudh 'elmiftaaH werooH.   خذ المفتاح وروح.
- khudh 'elqifl meAe 'elmiftaaH kemaan.   خذ القفل مع المفتاح كمان.
- helseqf Aaa·lee (high) ketheer.   هسقف عالي.
- helHaa'iT naa·See (low) shweyeh.   هلحايط ناصي شوية.
- 'elsiyaaj mde·wer (round).   السياج مدور.
- khudh Hemmaam webeAdeyn teAaal.   خذ حمام وبعدين تعال.
- rooH lilmeTbekh wejeeb shweyet 'ekl.   روح للمطبخ وجيب شوية اكل.
- helfurn mish ne·Zeef (clean).   هلفرن مش نظيف.
- 'il·Aeb (play) Taawlee.   العب طاولي.
- 'il·Aeb shiTrinj daa'imen.   العب شطرنج دائما.
- 'ilshiTrinj 'eHsen min (better than) 'elTewleee.   الشطرنج احسن من الطاولي.
- 'ilbes (wear) benTeloon 'eswad.   البس بنطلون اسود.

- fee maayoo b*i*helsooq 'ew maa fee?   في مايو بهسوق لو ما في؟
- helbaanyoo qe·deem (old).   هلبانيو قديم.
- metHef haa·di' (quiet).   متحف هادي.
- helqelem mish kweyyes.   هلقلم مش كويس.
- teAaal shoof heldefter.   تعال شوف هلدفتر.
- fee Saaboon b*i*helfindiq 'ew maa fee?   في صابون بهلفندق لو ما في؟
- '*e*lbe*y*t '*e*l'ebyeD mish bes b*i*emreekaa.   البيت الابيض مش بس بامريكا.
- '*e*lbenTeloon Teweel shweyeh.   البنطلون طويل شويه.
- helmeTbekh Segheer (small size) ketheer.   هلمطبخ صغير كثير.
- '*i*lkelb Segheer (small).   الكلب صغير.
- helkelb Semeen (fat).   هلكلب سمين.
- '*e*lweqt (the time) qe·Seer (short).   الوقت قصير.
- '*e*lmew·DooA (the subject) kaan (was) He·zeen (sad).   الموضوع كان حزين.
- heldefter thkheen.   هلدفتر ثخين.
- hel·shekhS (this person) leTeef (kind/soft).   هلشخص لطيف.
- helshekhS Ne·Heef (thin).   هالشخص نحيف.
- helshekhS mish De·Aeef (weak).   هلشخص مش ضعيف.
- helkelaam Te·reef (funny).   هلكلام طريف.
- '*e*lreesh (the feather) khe·feef (light).   الريش خفيف.
- helshekhS He·keem (wise).   هلشخص حكيم.
- helshaariA Ae·reeD (wide).   هلشارع عريض.
- helk*i*taab be·seeT (simple).   هلكتاب بسيط.
- helk*i*taab SeAb (difficult).   هلكتاب صعب.
- hel shaay Hi·loo (sweet).   هشي حلو.
- hel roob Dey·yiq (tight).   هروب ضيق.
- hel shaariA Deyyiq (narrow).   هشارع ضيق.
- helfilm kaan mum·tiA (joyful).   هلفلم كان ممتع.
- '*e*l'ekl bihelmeTAem se·ye' (bad).   الاكل بهل مطعم سيء.
- helsteeryoo be·Tee' (slow).   هلستيريو بطيء.
- haadhaa mej·noon (crazy).   هذا مجنون.
- haadhaa mef·tooH (opened).   هذا مفتوح.
- haadhaa mes·dood (closed).   هذا مسدود.
- haadhaa meH·boob (lovely)   هذا محبوب.
- haadhaa '*e*lblooz mu·reeH (comfortable).   هذا البلوز مريح.
- helkelaam meA·qool (logical).   هلكلام معقول.
- '*e*l'ez·req meAe '*e*l'eHmer jemeel.   الازرق مع الاحمر جميل.
- haak hel roob '*e*lwer·dee.   هاك هلروب الوردي.
- helHesheesh daa'imen '*e*kh·Der.   هلحشيش دائما اخضر.
- '*i*l·bes (wear) '*e*lbenTeloon '*e*lkhaa·kee.   البس البنطلون الخاكي.
- hel sheAr 'ebyeD (white hair).   هشعر ابيض.
- haadhaa 'esh·qer (blond).   هذا اشقر.
- haadhaa 'es·mer (brunette).   هذا اسمر.

Write these words using Arabic letters, as in teksee: تَكْسي

this/ this is: haa·dhaa _____
door: baab _____
market: sooq _____
chair: kur·see′ _____
kabob: ke′·baab _____

kabob: ke·baab′ _____
fish: se′·mek _____
please: min feD′·lek _____
the bill: ′elHi·saab′ _____

hello: mer·He·baa′ _____
safety: se·laa′·meh _____
yes: ′ey ′·weh _____
thanks: shuk·ren _____
good/okay: kwey′·yes _____
sugar: suk′·ker _____
or: ′ew _____

there exist/s: fee _____
but: laa′·kin _____
a little bit/some: shwe′·yeh _____
always: daa′·′i·men _____

not: mish _____
right/correct/true: Se·HeeH′ _____
also/more: ke·maan′ _____
take/grab: haak _____

eat: kul _____
make: sew·wee′ _____
buy: ′ish·ti·ree′ _____
money: floos _____

big/large/old in age: kebeer _____
black: ′es ′·wed _____
excellent: mum·taaz′ _____

by the means of/in: bi _____
bi′ ′el·′in·ke·lee′·zee _____
study: ′ud′·rus _____

taxi: tek·see′ ___تَكْسي___
home: beyt _____
book: kitaab′ _____
window: shu·baak′ _____
tea: shaa′·y _____

soup: soob _____
rice: ruzz _____
and: we- _____
bring: jeeb _____

with: me′·Ae _____
goodbye: me′·Ae ′el·se·laa′·meh _____
no: laa _____
you welcome/pardon: Aef·wen _____
tea: shaay _____
without: bi′·doon _____
the: ′el _____

there exist/s not: maa′ fee _____
a lot/very: ketheer _____
a little bit of: shwe′·yet _____

most likely: Het′·men _____
of course: Teb′·Aen _____
only/enough/but: bes _____

drink: ′ish ′·reb _____
cook: ′iT ′·bukh _____
let's/ come on: yel′·leh _____
and then: webeA·deyn′ _____

jacket/blazer: jaa′·keyt _____
beautiful: je·meel′ _____
delicious: le·dheedh′ _____

fast/in a hurry: bisur′·Aeh _____
bi′ ′el·Ae·re·bee′ _____
speak: ′it′·kel·lim _____

first/first of all: 'e·we·laan' _____   means: yeA·nee' _____
see: shoof _____

where: weyn _____	place: me·kaan' _____
close/near: qe·reeb' _____	close to: qe·reeb' min _____
go: rooH _____	come: te·Aaal' _____
bus: baaS _____	here: hi·naa' _____
there: hi·naak' _____	from: min _____
from the: mnil _____	to: li _____
to the: lil _____	bank: benk _____

travel: saa'·fir _____	visit: zoor _____
take: khudh _____	airport: me·Taar' _____
now: 'elaan _____	because: li'e'·ne·hu _____
for an example: me·the·len' _____	river: nehr _____
nehr 'el·neel' _____	museum: met'·Hef _____
theater: mes'·reH _____	film: film _____
The Middle East: 'el·sherq 'elaw'·seT _____ _____	

Make your own Sentences!

Use each of these words in a sentence or a phrase:

haadhaa هذا	merHebaa مَرْحَبا	'eyweh أَسْوَد
laa لا	shukren شُكْراً	Aefwen عفوا
minfeDlek من فضلك	kweyyes كويّس	kebaab كباب
soob سوب	semek سمك	meAe 'elselaameh مع السلامة
ruzz رزّ	shaay شاي	sukker سكر
elHisaab الحساب	we- وَ	'ew أو
'el ألـ	meAe مع	bidoon بدون
laakin لكن	daa'imen دائما	mish مش
Hetmen حتما	TebAen طبعا	kemaan كمان
bes بس	ketheer كثير	fee في
maa fee ما في	yelleh يله	webeAdeyn وبعدين
bi- بِـ	bil- بِلـ	fee في
min من	mnil- منل	li- لِـ
lil- لِلـ	'elaan الآن	li'e·ehu لأنهُ
yeAnee يعني	methelen مثلا	'ewelen اولا
weyn وين	taksee تكسي	baaS باص
baab باب	kursee كرسي	shubaak شباك
kitaab كتاب	floos فلوس	jaakeyt جاكيت
mekaan مكان	bayt بيت	sooq سوق
meTaar مطار	hinaa هنا	hinaak هناك
benk بنك	mesreH مسرح	metHef متحف
film فلم	nehr نهر	nehr 'elneel نهر النيل
ketheer كثير	kweyyes كويس	'elsherq 'elewseT الشرق الاوسط
shweyeh	shweyet شوية	SeHeeH صحيح

kebeer كبير	'eswed اسود	jemeel جميل
mumtaaz ممتاز	ledheedh لذيذ	qereeb قريب
qereeb min قريب من	bisurAeh بسرعة	bi'elAerebee بالعربي
bi'el'inkeleezee بالانكليزي	haak هاك	khudh خُذ
kul كُل	'ishreb اشرب	sewwee سوي
'iTbukh اطبخ	'ishtiree اشتري	shoof شوف
'udrus ادرس	'itkellim اتكلم	jeeb جيب
rooH روح	teAaal تعال	saafir سافر
zoor زور		

Practice Quiz

Translate the following learned lessons into Arabic:
1. This is a door.
2. Bring a chair please.
3. Bring rice and fish.
4. Kabob and rice.
5. Bring the bill.
6. Tea without sugar.
7. Hello, goodbye, yes, no.
8. Thanks, you are welcome, good.
9. Soup or fish?
10. Tea with sugar?
11. Good, good.
12. Bring the fish without the rice.
---
13. Is there soup?
14. Yes, there is.
15. No, there isn't.
26. There is no rice, but there is soup.
17. The soup is a lot, very much.
18. Always there is soup, always.
19. Bring a little bit of soup.
20. The kabob is a little bit.
---
21. Most likely, there is tea.
22. There is tea, but not a lot.
23. True or not true?
24. Take this book.
25. Of course, of course.
26. Enough sugar, enough, enough.
27. A bit more bit more sugar please.
28. The tea is good, but the sugar is not good.
---
29. Cook rice and then eat.
30. Drink tea.
31. Make money.
32. Come on buy a house.
33. Make fish and rice.
---

34. The house is big.
35. The big house.
36. The house is black.
37. The house is beautiful.
38. The book is excellent.
39. The kabob is delicious.

---

40. Talk in Arabic.
41. Talk fast.
42. Study this book.
43. First, bring the rice.
44. See the book.
45. This means, study Arabic in English.
46. Study and talk a lot.

---

47. Where is the house?
48. Where is the beautiful place?
49. The house is close.
50. The house is close to the market.
51. Go to the market.
52. Come here.
53. Come to the house, come.
54. Go from the bank to the house.
55. Go there.
56. Go from a place to place.
57. The house is not near the market.
58. The market is not close to here.
59. Go by bus, not by taxi.
60. Go by bus or by taxi.

---

61. Travel and visit the Middle East.
62. The Middle East is a very good place.
63. Go see the Nile River.
64. Take a bus and go visit the museum.
65. Take a taxi or a bus.
66. Go visit the museum because the museum is beautiful.
67. Go to the theater or go to the big mall (market).
68. Go see Arabic movie.
69. Come on, go see the river.
70. Come on, go to the airport fast.
71. The taxi is here come on go.
72. There is a good film, go see the film.
73. Take a bus and go.

You will need *The Arabic Alphabet for English Speakers by Camilia Sadik*:
- ✓ This textbook caters to the specific needs of English speakers.
- ✓ With meticulous transliteration, students begin to read from the first day of class.
- ✓ Arabic vowels, consonants, and nine Arabic symbols are dissected.
- ✓ Essential rules that govern the structure of Arabic words are discovered.
- ✓ No other methodology has 40+ original learning features in one program.
- ✓ It contains 800+ cognates.
- ✓ It is a class-tested approach.
- ✓ It works with or without a teacher.
- ✓ The author is a Linguist who dissected both English and Arabic.

Four Major Arabic Dialects أَرْبَع لَهجات رئيسِيَة

fuSHaw فُصْحى   Mediterranean لَهْجَة أَلْبَحْر أَلْمُتَوَسِط   Gulf لَهْجَة خَلِيجِيَة   Egyptian لَهْجَة مَصْرِيَة

Arabic speakers in 22 Arabian countries speak a countless number of dialects. However, and in addition to the formal form of Arabic (fuSHaw: فُصْحى), there are three major dialects spoken in the three major regions in the Middle East. Formal Arabic فُصْحى is usually used in formal speeches, on the news, and in all the written texts. Being that the Mediterranean countries are between Egypt and the Gulf Area, much of their dialect is a mixture of Gulf and Egyptian dialects.

The Egyptian dialect: أَلَّلهَجَة أَلْمَصْرِيَة
The Egyptian dialect is the most understood in all Arabian countries. This is due to the movie industry that flourished in Egypt since the 1950s and Arabic speakers watched Egyptian movies and they still do. If one is trying to learn spoken Arabic, it is safer to learn the Egyptian dialect. In this spoken Arabic book, the author picked the words that are most understood in every Arabian country, mostly Egyptian dialect is used. The last page in part one of this book, has a chart of all the learned words presented in the four major dialects. You may pick the dialect you wish to learn from the chart.

The following is a list of the Arabian countries and their Capitols: أَلدُوَل أَلْعَرَبِيَة وَعَواصِمَها.

The Gulf region dialect:

Iraq:	أَلعِراق	→	Baghdad:	بَغْداد
Kuwait:	أَلْكُوَيت	→	Kuwait:	أَلْكُوَيت
Saudi Arabia:	أَلسِعودِية	→	Riyadh:	أَلرِياض
Bahrain:	أَلْبَحرَين	→	Manama:	أَلْمَنامَة
Oman:	عُمان	→	Muscat:	مَسقَط
UAE:	ألإمارات	→	Abu Dhabi:	أبو ظَبي
Dubai:	دُبَي	→	Dubai:	دُبَي
Qatar:	قَطَر	→	Doha:	أَلدوحَة

The Mediterranean region dialect:

Lebanon:	لُبْنان	→	Beirut:	بَيْروت
Syria:	سورِيَة	→	Damascus:	دِمَشق
Jordan:	أَلأُردُن	→	Amman:	عَمان
Palestine:	فِلسْطين	→	Jerusalem:	أَلْقُدْس
Yemen:	أَليَمَن	→	Sana:	صَنْعاء
Aden:	عَدَن	→	Aden:	عَدَن

Egypt and Parts of Africa dialect:

Egypt:	مِصْر	→	Cairo:	أَلْقاهِرَة
Libya:	لِيبيا	→	Tripoli:	طَرَبلُس
Tunisia:	تونِس	→	Tunis:	تونِس
Algeria:	أَلْجَزائِر	→	Algeria:	أَلْجَزائِر
Morocco:	أَلْمَغرِب	→	Rabat:	أَلرِباط
Sudan:	أَلسودان	→	Khartoum:	أَلْخَرْطوم
Somalia:	أَلصومال	→	Mogadishu:	مَقْديشو
Djibouti:	جيبوتي	→	Djibouti:	جيبوتي
Mauritania:	موريتانيا	→	Nouakchott:	نَواكْشوط

The Four Major Arabic Dialects
Learned Words in the Four Major Dialects

You may choose your desired dialect and plug in the words you chose to use in the lessons above:

Learned Word	Egypt	Mediterranean	Gulf	FuSHaw
haa·dhaa هَذا	daa دا	hey·dhaa هَيْدا	haa·dhaa هَذا	haa·dhaa هَذا
sooq سوق	soo' سوء	soo' سوء	sook سوك	sooq سوق
kitaab كِتاب	ki·taab كِتاب	kitaab كْتاب	kitaab كْتاب	ki·taab كِتاب
shu·baak شُباك	shi·baak شِباك	shi·baak شِباك	shu·baak شُباك	shu·baak شُباك
soob سوب	soob/ shoor·beh	soob/ shoor·beh	soob/ shoor·beh	he·sse' حَساء
ruzz رُزّ	ruzz رُزّ	ruzz رُزّ	tim·men تِمَّن	ruzz رُزّ
min feDlek مِن فَضْلَك	min feDlek مِن فَضْلَك	min feDlek مِن فَضْلَك	ri·jaa·'en رجاءً	both are formal
'ey·weh أيْوَه	'ey·weh أيْوَه	be·laa بَلا	'ee ءي	ne·Aem نَعَم
kwey·yes كُوَيِّس	kwey·yes كُوَيِّس	Te·yib طَيِّب	zeyn زين	jey·id جَيِّد
suk·ker سُكَّر	suk·ker سُكَّر	suk·ker سُكَّر	she·ker شَكَر	suk·ker سُكَّر
bi·doon بِدون	bi·doon بِدون	bdoon/ be·laah بَلا	be·laa بَلا	bi·doon/ bi·laa بِدون
fee في	fee في	fee في	'e·koo أكو	yoo·jed يوجَد
maa fee ما في	me·feesh مَفيش	maa fee ما في	maa·koo ماكو	laa yoo·jed لا يوجَد
a lot: ketheer كَثير	ki·teer كِتير	kteer كْتير	hwaa·yeh هْوايَه	ke·theer كَثير
very: ketheer كَثير	'e·wee أوي	kteer كْتير	kul·lish گِلِّش	ji·den جِداً
mish مِش	mish مِش	moo مو	moo مو	ley·seh لَيْسَ
ke·maan كَمان	ke·maan كَمان	ke·maan كَمان	hem هَم	'ey·Den أيْضاً
kul كُل	kul كُل	kul كُل	'u·kul أكُل	kul كُل
jeeb جيب	geeb گيب	haat هات	jeeb جيب	haat هات
'ish·reb إشْرَب	'ish·reb إشْرَب	shraab شْراب	'ish·reb إشْرَب	'ish·reb إشْرَب
'iT·bukh إطْبُخ	'iT·bukh إطْبُخ	Tbukh طْبُخ	'uT·bukh أطْبُخ	'iT·hee إطْهي
'ish·ti·ree إشْتَري	shti·ree شْتَري	shti·ree شْتَري	shti·ree شْتَري	'ish·ti·ree إشْتَري
floos فْلوس	fi·loos فِلوس	me·Saa·ree مَصاري	floos فْلوس	ni·qood نِقود
kebeer كَبير	ki·beer كِبير	kebeer كَبير	chibeer جِبير	ke·beer كَبير
'es·wed أسْوَد	'is·wid إسْوِد	'es·wed أسْوَد	'es·wed أسْوَد	'es·wed أسْوَد
je·meel جَميل	ge·meel گَميل	je·meel جَميل	je·meel/ Hi·loo جَميل/ حلو	ja·meel جَميل
'it·kel·lim إتْكَلِّم	'it·kel·lim إتْكَلِّم	'iH·kee إحْكي	'iH·chee إحْجي	te·kel·lem تَكَلَّم
bisur·Aeh بِسُرْعَه	bisur·Aeh بِسُرْعَه	bisur·Aeh بِسُرْعَه	bisur·Aeh بِسُرْعَه	bi·sur·Ae·tin بِسُرْعَةٍ
weyn وَين	feyn فين	weyn وين	weyn وين	'eyn أيْن
qe·reeb قَريب	'e·reeb/ 'ureyib أريب	'e·reeb أريب	qe·reeb قَريب	qe·reeb قَريب
rooH روح	re·wiH رَوِح	rooH روح	rooH روح	'idh·heb إذْهَب
te·Aaal تَعال	teAaal/ teAaale تَعالا	jee جي	te·Aaal تَعال	te·Aaal تَعال
hi·naa هَنا	hi·naa هَنا	hoon/ hewnee هون	hnaa/ hnaaneh هْنا	hu·naa هُنا
hi·naak هِناك	hi·naak هِناك	hooneek هونيك	hnaak/ hnaakeh هْناك	hu·naak هُناك
khudh خُذ	khud خُد	khud خُد	'u·khudh أخُذ	khudh خُذ
haak هاك	haak هاك	haak هاك	haak هاك	
'elaan ألآن	dil we·'e·tee دِلْوَءْتي	he·laa هَلا	he·seh هَسَه	'el·aan ألآن
li·'e·ne·hu لأنَّهُ	li·'e·ne·hu لأنَّهُ	li·'e·noo لأنو	li·'e·ne·hu لأنَّهُ	li·'e·ne·hu لأنَّهُ
me·the·len مَثَلاً	me·se·len مَسَلاً	me·te·len مَثَلاً	me·the·len مَثَلاً	me·the·len مَثَلاً
nehr نَهْر	nehr نَهْر	ne·hir نَهِر	ne·her نَهَر	nehr نَهْر
film فِلْم	film فِلْم	fi·lim فِلِم	fi·lim فِلِم	film فِلْم
milH مِلْح	milH مِلْح	mi·liH مِلِح	mi·liH مِلِح	milH مِلْح
leHm لَحْم	leHm لَحْم	le·Him لَحِم	le·Hem لَحَم	leHm لَحْم

PART TWO
Verb Conjugations

Lesson 1: Verbs in command form (go to sleep: naam نام)

Lesson 2: I + verb (I sleep: 'enaa 'enaam أنا أنام)

Lesson 4: He + verb (He sleeps: huwe yenaam هو يَنام)

Lesson 5: We + verb (We sleep: neHnu nenaam نَحْن نَنام)

Lesson 6: She + verb (She sleeps: hiye tenaam هِيَ تَنام)

Lesson 7: You + verb (You sleep: inte tenaam إنْتَ تَنام)

Lesson 8: You (feminine) + verb (You sleep: inti tenaami إنْتِ تَنامِ)

Lesson 9: They + verb (They sleep: hum yenaamoon هُم يَنامون)

Lesson 10: Will + verb (He will sleep: huwe raaH yenaam هو راح يَنام)

Lesson 1 — Verbs in Command Form: الأفعال في صيغة الأمر

Spoken Arabic for English Speakers

❶ **Learning Step One:** Read aloud to memorize each word's sound and meaning. In Part One, no subjects were being introduced to avoid verb conjugation. In this part, all verbs are first introduced in a command form and in a masculine gender (you male go to sleep: naam نام):

sleep: naam	نام
get up: qoom	قوم
drink: 'ish'·reb	إِشْرَب
read: 'iq'·re*aa*'	إِقْرَأ
write: 'ik'·tub	إِكْتُب
speak: 'it'·kel·lem	إِتْكَلِّم
study: 'ud'·rus	أُدْرُس
work: 'ish'·ti·ghul	إِشْتِغُل
clean: neZ'·Zif	نَظِّف
love: Hib	حِب
play: 'il'·Aeb	إِلْعَب
enjoy: 'it'·me·teA	إِتْمَتَع
dream: 'iH'·lem	إِحْلَم
brush: 'if'·rish	إِفْرِش
give: 'iA·Tee'	إِعْطِي
eat: kul	كُل
take: khudh	خُذ
take a shower: knudh doosh	خُذ دوش
cut: 'iq'·TeA/qe'·tiA	إِقْطَع/ قَطِع
freeze something: fer'·zin	فَرْزِن
thaw something: dhew'·wib	ذَوِّب
come: jee' / te'·Aaal	جي/ تَعال
see: shoof	شوف

42

buy: 'ish'·tiree   إِشْتِري

make: sew'·wee   سَوّي

❷ Learning Step Two: Read aloud to learn the sentence pattern (verb in a command form):

naam fee 'ilbeyt.   نام في البَيت.
qoom min hinaa.   قوم مِن هِنا.
'ishreb shaay.   إِشرَب شاي.
'iqre*aa*' kitaab.   إِقرَأ كِتاب.
'iktub bilinkileezee.   إِكْتُب بِالإِنكِليزي.
'itkellem bilArebee.   إِتْكَلِّم بِالعَرَبي.
'udrus Arebee.   أُدْرُس عَرَبي.
'ishtughil fee 'elmeTAem.   إِشْتُغِل في المَطْعَم.
neZ'·Zif helmekaan.   نَظِّف هَلمَكان.
Hib daaimen.   حِب دائماً.
'ilAeb shweyeh.   إِلْعَب شويَه.
enjoy: 'itmeteA bilmetHef.   إِتْمَتَع بِالمَتحَف.
dream: 'iHlem bilArebee.   إِحْلَم بِالعَرَبي.
give: 'iATee floos.   إِعْطِي فلوس.
kul semek.   كُل سَمَك.
khudh floos.   خُذ فلوس.
knudh doosh.   خُذ دوش.
'iqTeA/qetiA 'ilkeyk.   إِقْطَع/ قَطِع الكَيْك.
ferzin 'illeHm.   فَرْزِن اللَحم.
dhewwib leHm 'ilkebaab.   ذَوِّب لَحم الكَباب.
jee/ teAaal hine.   جي/ تَعال هِنا.
'ishtiree dijaaj.   إِشْتِري دِجاج.
sewwee ruzz.   سَوِّي رُزّ.

❸ Learning Step Three: Speak aloud with new and old sentence patterns.
❹ Learning Step Four: Write as many sentences as you can remember.

Lesson 2   I + Verb: I sleep: 'enaa 'enaam   أنا أنام

❶ Learning Step One: Read aloud to memorize each word's sound and meaning. The subject here is the (I: 'enaa أنا). The verb is originally in a command form like (sleep: naam نام) and then it's conjugates to (I sleep: 'enaa 'enaam أنا أنام). Notice the conjugated verb begins with 'e أ to match the 'e أ in 'enaa أنا. In fact, ('enaam أنام) alone is enough to express that it is the ('enaa أنا) that sleeps. So, "I sleep" can be expressed like ('enaa 'enaam أنا أنام) or ('enaam أنام), without the 'enaa أنا.

I: 'e·naa'	أنا
see: shoof (v. in command form)	شوف.
I see: 'enaa 'e·shoof'.	أنا أشوف.
I see: 'eshoof.	أشوف.
I want: 'enaa 'e·reed'.	أنا أريد.
I want to see: 'enaa 'ereed 'eshoof.	أنا أريد أشوف.
I want to see: 'ereed 'eshoof.	أريد أشوف.
I sleep: 'enaa 'e·naam'.	أنا أنام.
I sleep: 'enaam.	أنام.
I get up: 'enaa 'e·qoom'.	أنا أقوم.
I drink: 'enaa 'esh'·reb.	أنا أشرَب.
I read: 'enaa 'eq'·re*aa*'.	أنا أقرأ.
I write: 'enaa 'ek'·tub.	أنا أكْتُب.
I speak: 'enaa 'et'·kel·lim.	أنا أتْكَلِّم.
I study: 'enaa 'ed'·rus.	أنا أدْرُس.
I work: 'enaa 'esh'·tug·hil.	أنا أشْتُغِل.
I clean: 'enaa 'e'·neZ·Zif.	أنا أنَظِف.
I love: 'enaa 'e'·Hib.	أنا أحِب.
I enjoy: 'enaa 'et'·me·teA.	أنا أتْمَتَع.
I dream: 'enaa 'eH'·lem.	أنا أحْلَم.
I give: 'enaa 'eA·Tee'.	أنا أعْطي.
I eat: 'enaa 'aa'·kul.	أنا آكُل.

I take: 'enaa 'aa' khudh.	أَنا آخُذ.
'enaa 'aakhudh doosh.	أَنا آخُذ دوش.
I cut: 'enaa 'e'·qe·TiA.	أَنا أَقطِع.
I freeze: 'enaa 'e'·fer·zin.	أَنا أَفرْزِن.
I thaw: 'enaa 'e'·dhew·wib.	أَنا أَذَوِّب.
I come: 'enaa 'e·jee'.	أَنا أَجي.
I mean: 'enaa 'eA·nee'.	أَنا أَعْني.
I buy: 'enaa 'esh·ti·ree'.	أَنا أَشْتِري.
I do: 'enaa 'ef'·Ael.	أَنا أَفْعَل.
I want to buy: 'e·reed 'eshtiree.	أَريد أَشْتِري.
I want to make: 'ereed 'e sew·wee'.	أَريد أَسَوّي.

'enaa 'eshoof beyt. 'enaa 'eshoof baab. 'enaa 'eshoof meTAem. 'enaa 'eshoof meTaar. 'enaa 'eshoof shaariA. 'enaa 'eshoof findiq. 'enaa 'eshoof teksee. 'enaa 'eshoof semek.

أَنا أَشوف بَيت. أَنا أَشوف باب. أَنا أَشوف مَطعَم. أَنا أَشوف مَطار. أَنا أَشوف شارع. أَنا أَشوف فِندِق. أَنا أَشوف تَكسي. أَنا أَشوف سَمَك.

➤We don't have to use 'enaa أنا because the verb is already conjugated from a command form (shoof شوف) to ('eshoof أشوف). Both the 'enaa أنا and the verb 'eshoof أشوف begin with 'e أ.

'eshoof beyt. 'eshoof baab. 'eshoof meTAem. 'eshoof meTaar. 'eshoof shaariA. 'eshoof findiq. 'eshoof teksee. 'eshoof semek.

أَشوف بَيت. أَشوف باب. أَشوف مَطعَم. أَشوف مَطار. أَشوف شارع. أَشوف فِندِق. أَشوف تَكسي. أَشوف سَمَك.

More words with (I + something):

name: 'ism	إِسْم
my name: 'is·mee'	إِسْمي
my name is Jack: 'ismee jaak.	إِسْمي جاك.
I am Jack (I jack): 'e·naa' jaak.	أَنا جاك.
I am Sue (I Sue): 'e·naa' soo.	أَنا سو.
I am happy: 'e·naa' fer·Haan'.	أَنا فَرْحان.
the one that: 'il·lee'	إِلْلي
must/necessary: laa'·zim	لازِم
inside/ in: prefix bi-	بِ
bigger/larger than the: 'ek'·ber mnil	أَكْبَر مِنل
that/that is: he·dhaak'	هَذاك

❷ Learning Step Two: Read aloud to learn the sentence pattern (I + verb + something):

'enaa 'ejeeb ruzz.	أَنا أَجيب رُزّ.
'enaa 'esewwee shaay.	أَنا أَسَوّي شاي.
'enaa 'eshreb shaay.	أَنا أَشْرَب شاي.
'enaa laa 'edrus Hisaab.	أَنا لا أَدْرُس حِساب.
'enaa 'etkellem ketheer.	أَنا أَتْكَلَّم كَثير.
'enaa 'erooH lilsooq.	أَنا أَروح لِلسوق.
'enaa 'ejee lilbeyt daa'imen.	أَنا أَجي لِلْبَيت دائِماً.
'enaa daa'imen 'esaafir.	أَنا دائِماً أَسافِر.
daa'imen 'enaa 'ezoor 'elmetHef.	دائِماً أَنا أَزور أَلْمَتْحَف.
'enaa 'etkellem shweyet Aerebee.	أَنا أَتْكَلِّم شْوَيَة عَرَبي.
'enaa 'ereed semek weruzz.	أَنا أَريد سَمَك وَرُزّ.
'ereed shaay wekeyk kemaan.	أَريد شاي وَكَيْك كَمان.
laazim 'eshoof mekaan kebeer.	لازِم أَشوف مَكان كَبير.
helfindiq mish kebeer.	هَلْفِنْدِق مِش كَبير.
'ereed mekaan 'ekber mnilfindiq.	أَريد مكان أَكْبَر مْنِلْفِنْدِق.

hidhaak findiq kebeer.   هِناك فِنْدِق كَبير.
'enaa 'ejeeb shaay wekeyk.   أنا أجيب شاي وكَيْك.
'ejeeb shaay wekeyk.   أجيب شاي وأجيب كَيْك.
'enaa 'illee 'ejeeb 'ilshaay we'elkeyk.   أنا إِلْلي أجيب أَلْشاي وأَلْكَيك.
'enaa 'illee daa'men 'ejeeb shaay wekeyk.   أنا إِلْلي دائِماً أجيب شاي وكَيك.
TebAen 'enaa 'illee 'esewwee 'ilshaay.   طَبْعاً أنا إِلْلي أسَوّي أَلْشاي.
'eyweh laazim 'esewwee 'ilshaay.   أيْوَه لازِم أسَوّي أَلْشاي.

> Learn these prepositions:
to: 'i'·law إلى
to the: 'ilaw 'el إلى أَلْـ
I go to the: 'erooH 'ilaw 'el أروح إلى أَلْـ
I travel to the: 'esaafir 'ilaw 'el أسافِر إلى أَلْ
from: min مِن
from the: min 'el/minil/ mnil مِن أَلْ/ مِنِل/ منِل
I am from Iraq: 'enaa mnil 'iraaq أنا مِن أَلْعِراق
I came from Iraq: 'enaa 'ejee mnil 'iraaq أنا أجي مِن أَلْعِراق

'enaa 'erooH 'ilaw 'elbeyt. 'erooH lilmeTaar. 'esaafir 'ilaw miSr. 'enaa 'erooH wejee min 'emreekaa 'ilaw miSr. miSr 'um 'ildunyaa.

أنا أروح إلى أَلْبَيت. أروح لِلْمَطار. أسافِر إلى مِصر. أنا أروح وَجي مِن أَمْريكا إلى مِصْر. مِصر أم أَلْدُنْيا.

Read more sentence patterns for extra practice:

'enaa 'illee 'eTbukh, bes mish daa'imen. 'ewelen, laazim 'eshoof findiq bhelshaariA. 'ereed 'eshtiree beyt kebeer. 'ereed beyt kebeer li'enehu 'ereed 'esewwee mesreH fee 'elbeyt. yeAnee 'ereed 'eshtiree beyt 'ekber min helbeyt.

أنا إِللي أطْبُخ، بس مِش دائِماً. أوَلاً، لازم أشوف فِنْدِق بِهَلْشارِع. أريد أشْتِري بَيت كَبير. أريد بَيت كَبير لِأنَه أريد أسَوّي مَسْرَح في ألْبَيت. يَعْني أريد أشْتِري بَيت أكْبَر مِنْ هَلْبَيت.

'ereed 'esaafir. laa 'ereed beyt, welaa 'ereed mekaan kebeer. 'ereed 'eshoof 'ilshaariA 'elqereeb min nehr 'ilneel. TebAen, 'ereed 'eshoof 'elsemek bilmey. 'ereed 'eshreb mey nehr 'ilneel. 'ereed 'erooH lilsooq 'elqedeem. 'ereed 'eshoof film kweyyis. 'ereed 'ejeeb kebaab; laa, laa 'ereed kebaab. 'ereed 'aakul semek weruzz 'elaan.

أريد أسافِر، لا أريد بَيت وَلا أريد مَكان كَبير. أريد أشوف إلْشارِع ألْقَريب مِن نَهر إلنيل. طَبْعاً، أريد أشوف ألْسَمَك بِلْمَي. أريد أشْرَب مَي نَهر إلنيل. أريد أروح لِلْسوق ألْقَديم. أريد أشوف فِلم كوَّيس. أريد أجيب كَباب؛ لا، لا أريد كَباب. أريد آكُل سَمَك وَرُزّ ألآن.

➤ The verbs "take" and "eat" conjugate differently. (I take: 'aa′ khudh آخُذ) and (I eat: 'aa′ kul آكُل).
'enaa 'aakhudh Arebee bilinkileezee: أنا آخُذ عَرَبي بِالإنْكِليزي
'ereed 'aakhudh teksee: أريد آخُذ تِكسي
'ereed 'aakul fee 'ilsooq: أريد آكُل في ألْسوق
'enaa laa 'aakul keyk welaa 'aakul beqlaaweh: أنا لا آكُل كَيك ولا آكُل بَقْلاوَة

❸ Learning Step Three: Speak aloud with new and old sentence patterns.
❹ Learning Step Four: Write as many sentences as you can remember.

Lesson 3   He + Verb هُوَ يَنام   Spoken Arabic for English Speakers

❶ Learning Step One: Read aloud to memorize each word's sound and meaning:

he:	hu′·we	هُوَ
one/someone (m.):	waa′·Hid	واحِد
guy:	shekhS	شَخْص/رَجُل
human being:	'in·saan'	إنْسان
Adam:	'aa'·dem	آدَم
Sam:	saam	سام
Jamal:	je·maal'	جَمال
Jack:	jaak	جاك
George:	jōorj	جورج
Arabian (masculine):	Ae·re·bee'	عَرَبي
Russian (masculine):	roo′·see	روسي
American:	'em·ree·kee'	أمْريكي
teacher (masculine):	mu′·Ael·lim	مُعَلِّم
actor:	mu′·me·thil	مُمَثِّل
doctor:	dik·tōor'	دِكْتور
employee:	mu′·we·Zef	مُوَظَّف
chef (masculine):	Te·baakh'	طَباخ
dog (masculine):	kelb	كَلْب
was (masculine):	kaan	كان

Verb Conjugations

command form verb		he + verb	
bring: jeeb	جيب	yejeeb	هُوَ يَجيب
sleep: naam	نام	yenaam	هُوَ يَنام
see: shoof	شوف	yeshoof	هُوَ يَشوف
get up: qoom	قوم	yeqoom	هُوَ يَقوم

The "e" in "ye-" is usually silent in spoken Arabic but not in formal Arabic.

he brings: huwe y*e*jeeb	هُوَ يجيب
Jamal sees: jemaal y*e*shoof	جَمال يشوف
Sam goes: Sam y*e*rooH	سام يروح
Adam visits: aadem y*e*zoor	آدَم يزور

❷ Learning Step Two: Read aloud to learn the sentence pattern (he + verb + something):

huwe y*e*jeeb ruzz.	هُوَ يجيب رُزّ.
huwe y*e*sewwee shaay.	هُوَ يسَوّي شاي.
huwe y*e*shreb shaay.	هُوَ بِشْرَب شاي.
huwe laa y*e*drus Hisaab.	هُوَ لا يدْرُس حِساب.
huwe y*e*tkellem ketheer.	هُوَ بِتْكَلِّم كَثير.
huwe y*e*rooH lilsooq.	هُوَ يروح لِلْسوق.
huwe y*e*jee lilbeyt daa'imen.	هُوَ يجي لِلْبَيت دائِماً.
huwe daa'imen y*e*saafir.	هُوَ دائِماً يسافِر.
daa'imen huwe y*e*zoor 'elmetHef.	دائِماً هُوَ يزور ألْمَتْحَف.
huwe y*e*tkellem shweyet Aerebee.	هُوَ بِتْكَلِّم شْوَيَة عَرَبي.
huwe y*e*reed semek weruzz.	هُوَ يريد سَمَك وَرُزّ.
y*e*reed shaay wekeyk kemaan.	يريد شاي وَكَيْك كَمان.
laazim y*e*shoof mekaan kebeer.	لازم يشوف مَكان كَبير.
helfindiq mish kebeer.	هَلْفِنْدِق مِش كَبير.
y*e*reed mekaan 'ekber mnilfindiq.	يريد مكان أَكْبَر مْنِلْفِنْدِق.
hidhaak findiq kebeer.	هِناك فِنْدِق كَبير.
huwe y*e*jeeb shaay wekeyk.	هُوَ يجيب شاي وكَيْك.
y*e*jeeb shaay wekeyk.	يجيب شاي ويجيب كَيْك.
huwe 'illee y*e*jeeb 'ilshaay we'elkeyk.	هُوَ إِلْلي يجيب ألْشاي وَألْكَيْك.
huwe 'illee daa'men y*e*jeeb shaay wekeyk.	هُوَ إِلْلي دائِماً يجيب شاي وكَيْك.
TebAen huwe 'illee y*e*sewwee 'ilshaay.	طَبْعاً هُوَ إِلْلي يسَوّي ألْشاي.
'eyweh laazim y*e*sewwee 'ilshaay.	أَيْوَه لازِم يسَوّي ألْشاي.
waaHid roosee y*e*tkellem Aerebee.	واحِد روسي بِتْكَلِّم عَرَبي.
haadhaa shekhS kweyyis.	هَذا شَخْص كِوَّيِس.
aadem y*e*drus fee miSr.	آدَم يدْرُس في مَصر.

saam yishtughil muweZef. سام بِشْتُغِل مُوَظَف.
jemaal yeHub 'ilshaay. جَمال يحب أَلْشاي.
jaak Tebaakh yeTbukh 'ekl ledheedh جاك طَباخ يطبُخ أكْل لَذيذ.
joorj yaakul 'ekl Aerebee جورج ياكُل أكْل عَرَبي.
'ilmumethil kaan muAellim. إِلْمُمَثِل كان مُعَلِّم.
'ilkelb 'emreekee weyerooH lildiktoor. إِلْكَلْب أَمْريكي وَيروح لِلْدِكْتور.

Verb Conjugations

command form verb	he + verb
bring: jeeb جيب	yejeeb هُوَ يجيب
sleep: naam نام	yenaam هُوَ ينام
see: shoof شوف	yeshoof هُوَ يشوف
get up: qoom قوم	yeqoom هُوَ يقوم
go: rooH روح	yerooH هُوَ يروح
put: HuT حُط	yeHut هُوَ يحُط
love: Hib حِب	yeHib هُوَ يحِب
feel: Hiss حِس	yeHis هُوَ يحِس
think: fekir فَكِر	yefekir هُوَ يفَكِر
cut: qeTiA قَطِع	yeqeTiA هُوَ يقَطِع
thaw: dhewwib ذَوِّب	yedhewwib هُوَ يذَوِّب
do/make: sewwee سَوّي	yesewwee هُوَ يسَوّي
come: teAaal/jee تَعال/ جي	yejee هُوَ يجي
study: 'udrus أُدْرُس	yedrus هُوَ يِدرُس
eat: kul كُل	yaakul هُوَ ياكُل
take: khudh خُذ	yaakhudh هُوَ ياخُذ
take/grab: haak هاك	

As in 'ishreb إِشْرَب, when the verb in a command form begins with ('i إِ) the ('i إِ) is not silent and it stays when conjugated, as in (he drinks: yishreb هُوَ بِشرَب):

drink: 'ishreb إِشْرَب	yishreb هُوَ بِشرَب
work: 'ishtughul إِشْتُغْل	yishtughul هُوَ بِشْتُغْل
buy: 'ishteree إِشْتِري	yishteree هُوَ بِشْتِري
talk: 'iHkee إحْكي	yiHkee هُوَ بِحكي
need: 'iHtaaj إحْتاج	yiHtaaj هُوَ بِحْتاج

walk: 'imshee إِمْشِي   yimshee هُوَ بِمْشِي
play: 'ilAeb إِلْعَب   yilAeb هُوَ بِلْعَب
speak: 'itkellim إِتْكَلِّم   yitkellim هُوَ بِتْكَلِّم
give: 'iATee إِعْطِي   yiATee هُوَ بِعْطِي
mean: 'iAnee إِعْنِي   yeiAnee هُوَ بِعْنِي
enjoy: 'itmeteA إِتْمَتَع   yitmeteA هُوَ بِتْمَتَع
read: 'iqraae' بِقْرَأ   yiqraae' هُوَ بِقْرَأ
use: 'isteAmil إِسْتَعْمِل   yisteAmil هُوَ بِسْتَعْمِل
hear: 'ismeA إِسْمَع   yismeA هُوَ بِسْمَع
write: 'iktib إِكْتِب   yiktib هُوَ بِكْتِب
request: 'iTlub إِطْلُب   yiTlub هُوَ بِطْلُب

Read more sentence patterns for extra practice:

huwa 'illee yeTbukh, bes mish daa'imen. 'ewelen, laazim yeshoof findiq bhelshaariA. yereed yeshtiree beyt kebeer. yereed beyt kebeer li'enehu yereed yesewwee mesreH fee 'elbeyt. yeAnee yereed yeshtiree beyt 'ekber min helbeyt.

هُوَ إِلْلِي يطْبُخ، بَس مِش دائِماً. أَوَلاً، لازِم يشوف فِنْدِق بِهَلْشارع. يريد يشْتِري بَيت كَبير. يريد بَيت كَبير لِأَنَّه يريد يسَوّي مَسْرَح في أَلْبَيت. يَعْني يريد يشْتِري بَيت أَكْبَر مِنْ هَلْبَيت.

yereed yesaafir. laa yereed beyt, welaa yereed mekaan kebeer. bes yereed yeshoof 'ilshaariA 'elqereeb min nehr 'ilneel. TebAen, yereed yeshoof yelsemek bilmey. yereed yishreb mey nehr 'ilneel. yereed yerooH lilsooq 'elqedeem. yereed yeshoof film kweyyis. yereed yejeeb kebaab; laa, laa yereed kebaab. yereed yaakul semek weruzz 'elaan.

يريد يسافِر، لا يريد بَيت وَلا يريد مَكان كَبير. بَس يريد يشوف إِلْشارع أَلْقَريب مِن نَهر إِلنيل. طَبْعاً، يريد يشوف أَلْسَمَك بِلْمَي. يريد بِشْرَب مَي نَهر إِلنيل. يريد يروح لِلسوق أَلْقَديم. يريد يشوف فِلم كَوّيس. يريد يجيب كَباب؛ لا، لا يريد كَباب. يريد ياكُل سَمَك وَرُزّ أَلآن.

❸ Learning Step Three: Speak aloud with new and old sentence patterns.
❹ Learning Step Four: Write as many sentences as you can remember.

Lesson 4   We + Verb نَحْنُ نَنام   Spoken Arabic for English Speakers

❶ Learning Step One: Read aloud to memorize each word's sound and meaning:

we (different dialects): neH′·nu نَحْنُ / ʾih′·ne إحْنَ / ni′·Hne نِحْنُ
we sleep: neH′·nu ne·naam′   نَحْنُ نَنام
we see: neH′·nu neshoof′   نَحْنُ نشوف
we sleep: neH′·nu ne·naam′   نَحْنُ نَنام
we bring: neH′·nu nejeeb   نَحْنُ نجيب
people: naas   ناس
we're people: naas   نَحْنُ ناس
still: li′ seh   لِسه
not yet: liseh laa   لِسه لا
not a problem: mish mush′ ki leh   مِش مُشْكِلَة
certainly: ʿe·keed   أَكيد
congratulations: meb·rook′   مَبْروك
very: ji′·den   جِداً
office: ʿōo′ fees   أوْفيس
helicopter: hi li kōob′ ter   هِلِكوبْتَر
the pyramids: ʿel ʿeh raam′   ألأهْرام

Verb Conjugations

We usually add the prefix (ne نَ) to a verb to conjugate it from the command form as in (shoof شوف) to (neHnu neshoof نَحْنُ نشوف). The prefix "ne" in the conjugated verb matches the "ne" in "neHnu".

command form verb	we + verb
bring: jeeb جيب	nejeeb نَحْنُ نجيب
sleep: naam نام	nenaam نَحْنُ نَنام
see: shoof شوف	neshoof نَحْنُ نشوف
get up: qoom قوم	neqoom نَحْنُ نقوم
go: rooH روح	nerooH نَحْنُ نروح
put: HuT حُط	neHut نَحْنُ نحُط

love: Hib حِب	neHib نَحْنُ نحِب
feel: Hiss حِس	neHis نَحْنُ نحِس
think: fekir فَكِر	nefekir نَحْنُ نفَكِر
cut: qeTiA قَطِع	neqeTiA نَحْنُ نقَطِع
thaw: dhewwib ذَوِّب	nedhewwib نَحْنُ نذَوِّب
do/make: sewwee سَوِّي	nesewwee نَحْنُ نسَوِّي
come: teAaal/jee تَعال/ جي	nejee نَحْنُ نجي
study: 'udrus أُدْرُس	nedrus نَحْنُ ندرُس
eat: kul كُل	naakul نَحْنُ ناكُل
take: khudh خُذ	naakhudh نَحْنُ ناخُذ
take/grab: haak هاك	

As in 'ishreb إِشْرَب, when the verb in a command form begins with ('i إِ) the ('i إِ) is not silent and it stays when conjugated to (we drink: nishreb نَحْنُ نِشرَب):

drink: 'ishreb إِشْرَب	nishreb نَحْنُ نِشرَب
work: 'ishtughul إِشْتُغُل	nishtughul نَحْنُ نِشْتُغُل
buy: 'ishteree إِشْتِري	nishteree نَحْنُ نِشْتِري
talk: 'iHkee إِحْكي	niHkee نَحْنُ نِحكي
need: 'iHtaaj إِحْتاج	niHtaaj نَحْنُ نِحْتاج
walk: 'imshee إِمْشي	nimshee نَحْنُ نِمْشي
play: 'ilAeb إِلْعَب	nilAeb نَحْنُ نِلْعَب
speak: 'itkellim إِتكَلِّم	nitkellim نَحْنُ نِتْكَلِّم
give: 'iATee إِعْطي	niATee نَحْنُ نِعْطي
mean: 'iAnee إِعْني	neiAnee نَحْنُ نِعْني
enjoy: 'itmeteA إِتْمَتَع	nitmeteA نَحْنُ نِتْمَتَع
read: 'iqraae' نِقْرَأ	niqraae' نَحْنُ نِقْرَأ
use: 'isteAmil إِسْتَعْمِل	nisteAmil نَحْنُ نِسْتَعْمِل
hear: 'ismeA إِسْمَع	nismeA نَحْنُ نِسْمَع
write: 'iktib إِكْتِب	niktib نَحْنُ نِكْتِب
request: 'iTlub إِطْلُب	niTlub نَحْنُ نِطْلُب

❷ Learning Step Two: Read aloud to learn the sentence pattern (we + verb + something):

neHnu nejeeb ruzz. نَحْنُ نجيب رُزّ.
neHnu nesewwee shaay. نَحْنُ نسَوِّي شاي.

neHnu nishreb shaay.	نَحْنُ نِشْرَب شَايِ.
neHnu laa nedrus Hisaab.	نَحْنُ لا ندْرُس حِساب.
neHnu nitkellem ketheer.	نَحْنُ نِتْكَلِّم كَثير.
neHnu nerooH lilsooq.	نَحْنُ نروح لِلْسوق.
neHnu nejee lilbeyt daa'imen.	نَحْنُ نجي لِلْبَيت دائِماً.
neHnu daa'imen nesaafir.	نَحْنُ دائِماً نسافِر.
daa'imen neHnu nezoor 'elmetHef.	دائِماً نَحْنُ نزور أَلْمَتْحَف.
neHnu nitkellem shweyet Aerebee.	نَحْنُ نِتْكَلِّم شْوَيَة عَرَبِي.
neHnu nereed semek weruzz.	نَحْنُ نريد سَمَك وَرُزّ.
nereed shaay wekeyk kemaan.	نريد شاي وَكَيْك كَمان.
laazim neshoof mekaan kebeer.	لازِم نشوف مَكان گَبير.
helfindiq mish kebeer.	هَلْفِنْدِق مِش گَبير.
nereed mekaan 'ekber mnilfindiq.	نريد مكان أَكْبَر مْنِلْفِنْدِق.
hidhaak findiq kebeer.	هِناك فِنْدِق گَبير.
neHnu nejeeb shaay wekeyk.	نَحْنُ نجيب شاي وكَيْك.
nejeeb shaay wekeyk.	نجيب شاي ونجيب كَيْك.
neHnu 'illee nejeeb 'ilshaay we'elkeyk.	نَحْنُ إلْلي نجيب أَلْشاي وأَلْكَيك.
neHnu 'illee daa'men nejeeb keyk.	نَحْنُ إلْلي دائِماً نجيب كَيك.
TebAen neHnu 'illee nesewwee 'ilshaay.	طَبْعاً نَحْنُ إلْلي نسَوّي أَلْشاي.
'eyweh laazim nesewwee 'ilshaay.	أَيْوَه لازِم نسَوّي أَلْشاي.
'enaa wewaaHid roosee nitkellem Aerebee.	أنا وَواحِد روسي نِتكَلَّم عَرَبِي.
neHnu naas kweyyiseen jiden.	نَحْنُ ناس كِوَّيسين جِداً.
mebrook neHnu nitkillim Aerebee	مَبْروك نَحْنُ نِتْكَلِّم عَرَبِي.
'enaa weaadem nedrus fee miSr.	أنا وآدَم ندرُس في مَصر.
'enaa wehuwe neshoof 'il'ehraam.	أنا وهُوَ نشوف الأهْرام.
'enaa wejemaal nejeeb mey.	أنا وجمال نجيب مَي.
neHnu liseh nishteghil fee 'iloofees.	نَحنُ لِسَه نِشْتِغِل في الأوفيس.
neHnu liseh laa naakul leHm.	نَحْنُ لِسَه لا ناكُل لَحم.
neHnu neHib'ilshaay.	نَحْنُ نحب أَلْشاي.
neHnu neTbukh 'ekl ledheedh	نَحْنُ نطبُخ أَكْل لَذيذ.

❸ Learning Step Three: Speak aloud with new and old sentence patterns.
❹ Learning Step Four: Write as many sentences as you can remember.

Lesson 5 — She + Verb هِيَ تَنام

❶ **Learning Step One:** Read aloud to memorize each word's sound and meaning:

she: hi´·ye	هِيَ
Nadia: naa´·di·yaa	ناديا
je·mee´·leh (female name)	جَميلَة
ley´·law (f. name)	لَيلى
language: lu´·gheh (f.)	لُغَة
human being (male): in·saan´	إنْسان
human being (female): in·saa´·neh	إنْسانَة
a country (f.): de´·wleh	دَوْلَة
important (m.): mu´·him	مُهِم
important (f.): mu´·hi·meh	مُهِمَة
balcony: baal´·kōon	بالْكون
a dress: fus·taan´	فُسْتان
she wears: hiya til´·bes	هِيَ تِلْبَس
she sleeps: tenaam´	تنام
she sees: hiya teshoof´	هِيَ تشوف
she brings: hiya tejeeb	هِيَ تجيب

Verb Conjugations

We usually add the prefix (te تَـ) to conjugate a verb from a command form as in (shoof شوف) to (hiye teshoof هِيَ تشوف):

command form verb	she + verb
bring: jeeb جيب	tejeeb هِيَ تجيب
sleep: naam نام	tenaam هِيَ تنام
see: shoof شوف	teshoof هِيَ تشوف
get up: qoom قوم	teqoom هِيَ تقوم
go: rooH روح	terooH هِيَ تروح
put: HuT حُط	teHut هِيَ تحُط
love: Hib حِب	teHib هِيَ تحِب

feel: Hiss حِس	هِيَ تحِس teHiss
think: fekir فَكِر	هِيَ تفَكِر tefekir
cut: qeTiA قَطِع	هِيَ تقَطِع teqeTiA
thaw: dhewwib ذَوِّب	هِيَ تذَوِّب tedhewwib
do/make: sewwee سَوّي	هِيَ تسَوّي tesewwee
come: teAaal/jee تَعال/ جي	هِيَ تجي tejee
study: 'udrus أُدْرُس	هِيَ تدرُس tedrus
eat: kul كُل	هِيَ تاكُل taakul
take: khudh خُذ	هِيَ تاخُذ taakhudh
take/grab: haak هاك	هاكي haakee

As in 'ishreb إِشْرَب, when the verb in a command form begins with ('i إِ) the ('i إِ) is not silent and it stays when conjugated to (she drinks: tishreb هِيَ تِشرَب):

drink: 'ishreb إِشْرَب	هِيَ تِشرَب tishreb
work: 'ishtughul إِشْتُغُل	هِيَ تِشْتُغُل tishtughul
buy: 'ishteree إِشْتِري	هِيَ تِشتِري tishteree
talk: 'iHkee إِحْكي	هِيَ تِحكي tiHkee
need: 'iHtaaj إِحْتاج	هِيَ تِحْتاج tiHtaaj
walk: 'imshee إِمْشي	هِيَ تِمْشي timshee
play: 'ilAeb إِلْعَب	هِيَ تِلْعَب tilAeb
speak: 'itkellim إِتكَلِّم	هِيَ تِتْكَلِّم titkellim
give: 'iATee إِعْطي	هِيَ تِعْطي tiATee
mean: 'iAnee إِعني	هِيَ تِعْني tiAnee
enjoy: 'itmeteA إِتْمَتَع	هِيَ تِتْمَتَع titmeteA
read: 'iqraae' تِقْرَأ	هِيَ تِقْرَأ tiqraae'
use: 'isteAmil إِسْتَعْمِل	هِيَ تِسْتَعْمِل tisteAmil
hear: 'ismeA إِسْمَع	هِيَ تِسْمَع tismeA
write: 'iktib إِكْتِب	هِيَ تِكْتِب tiktib
request: 'iTlub إِطْلُب	هِيَ تِطْلُب tiTlub

❷ Learning Step Two: Read aloud to learn the sentence pattern (she + verb + something):

hiye tejeeb ruzz.	هِيَ تجيب رُزّ.
hiye tesewwee shaay.	هِيَ تسَوّي شاي.

hiye tishreb shaay.	هِيَ تِشْرَب شاي.
hiye laa tedrus Hisaab.	هِيَ لا تِدْرُس حِساب.
hiye titkellem ketheer.	هِيَ تِتْكَلِّم كَثير.
hiye terooH lilsooq.	هِيَ تروح لِلْسوق.
hiye tejee lilbeyt daa'imen.	هِيَ تجي لِلْبَيت دائِماً.
hiye daa'imen tesaafir.	هِيَ دائِماً تسافِر.
daa'imen hiye tezoor 'elmetHef.	دائِماً هِيَ تزور أَلْمَتْحَف.
hiye titkellem shweyet Aerebee.	هِيَ تِتْكَلِّم شْوَيَة عَرَبي.
hiye tereed semek weruzz.	هِيَ تريد سَمَك وَرُزّ.
tereed shaay wekeyk kemaan.	تريد شاي وَكَيْك كَمان.
laazim teshoof mekaan kebeer.	لازم تشوف مَكان گبير.
helfindiq mish kebeer.	هَلْفِنْدِق مِش گبير.
tereed mekaan 'ekber mnilfindiq.	تريد مكان أَكْبَر مْنِلْفِنْدِق.
hidhaak findiq kebeer.	هِناك فِنْدِق گبير.
hiye tejeeb shaay wekeyk.	هِيَ تجيب شاي وكَيْك.
tejeeb shaay wekeyk.	تجيب شاي وتجيب كَيْك.
hiye 'illee tejeeb 'ilshaay we'elkeyk.	هِيَ إِلْلي تجيب أَلْشاي وأَلْكَيك.
hiye 'illee daa'men tejeeb keyk.	هِيَ إِلْلي دائِماً تجيب كَيْك.
TebAen hiye 'illee tesewwee 'ilshaay.	طَبْعاً هِيَ إِلْلي تسَوّي أَلْشاي.
'eyweh laazim tesewwee 'ilshaay.	أَيْوَه لازِم تسَوّي أَلْشاي.
naadiyaa tidrus fee 'ilbaalkōon.	نادِيا تِدْرُس في أَلْبالْكون.
jemeeleh tilbes fustaan jemeel.	جَميلَة تِلْبَس فُستان جَميل.
hiye teHib tesaafir lidewleh Aerebiyeh.	هِيَ تحب تسافِر لِدَولَة عَرَبِيَة.
leylaw 'insaaneh muhimeh.	ليلى إِنسانَة مُهِمَة جِداً.
hiye tiktib kitaab lugheh.	هِيَ تِكْتِب كِتاب لُغَة.
mebrook leylaw.	مَبْروك لَيلى.

➤ Note that when you ask Arabic speakers for the meaning of a verb, they immediately tell you the masculine form of that verb. For instance, you ask them for the meaning of "sleep" or "to sleep". There is answer is usually (yenaam يَنام). Ask them for the command form of that verb so you know how to conjugate it.

❸ Learning Step Three: Speak aloud with new and old sentence patterns.
❹ Learning Step Four: Write as many sentences as you can remember.

Lesson 6 — You + Verb إِنْتَ تَنَام

❶ Learning Step One: Read aloud to memorize each word's sound and meaning:

you (masculine)	'in'·te	إِنْتَ
you want	'inte tereed	إِنْتَ تريد
Do you want?	'inte tereed?	إِنْتَ تريد؟
I have	Ain·dee'	عِنْدي
mall	sooq/mōol	سوق/ مول
medication	de·waa''	دَواء
Aspirin	'es·pi·reen'	أَسْبِرين
toilet papers	we'·req ti·waa'·leyt	وَرَق تِواليت
penicillin	ben·se·leen'	بَنْسَلين
pain	'e'·lem	أَلَم
diabetes	suk'·ker	سُكَّر
AIDS test	feHA 'eydz	فَحْص أَيْدْز

Verb Conjugations

We usually add the prefix (te نَ) to conjugate a verb from a command form as in (shoof شوف) to ('inte **te**shoof إِنْتَ تشوف):

command form verb		she + verb	
bring: jeeb	جيب	tejeebi	إِنْتِ تجيب
sleep: naam	نام	tenaami	إِنْتَ تنام
see: shoof	شوف	teshoofi	إِنْتَ تشوف
get up: qoom	قوم	teqoomi	إِنْتَ تقوم
go: rooH	روح	terooHi	إِنْتَ تروح
put: HuT	حُط	teHuti	إِنْتَ تحُط
love: Hib	حِب	teHibi	إِنْتَ تحِب
feel: Hiss	حِس	teHisi	إِنْتَ تحِس
think: fekir	فَكِر	tefekiri	إِنْتَ تفَكِر
cut: qeTiA	قَطِع	teqeTiAi	إِنْتَ تقَطِع
thaw: dhewwib	ذَوِّب	tedhewwibi	إِنْتَ تذَوِّب

do/make: sewwee سَوّي	tesewweei إِنْتَ تسَوّي
come: teAaal/jee تَعال/ جي	tejeei إِنْتَ تجي
study: 'udrus أدْرُس	tedrusi إِنْتَ تدرُس
help: saaAid ساعِد	tesaaAidi إِنْتَ تساعَد
be: koon كون	tekooni إِنْتَ تكون
eat: kul كُل	taakuli إِنْتَ تاكُل
take: khudh خُذ	taakhudhi إِنْتَ تاخُذ
take/grab: haak هاك	haakee هاك

As in 'ishreb إشرَب, when the verb in a command form begins with ('i إ) the ('i إ) is not silent and it stays when conjugated to (you drink: tishreb إِنْتَ تِشرَب):

drink: 'ishreb إشرَب	tishreb إِنْتَ تِشرَب
work: 'ishtughul إشْتُغُل	tishtughul إِنْتَ تِشْتُغُل
buy: 'ishteree إشتِري	tishteree إِنْتَ تِشتِري
talk: 'iHkee إحكي	tiHkee إِنْتَ تِحكي
need: 'iHtaaj إحتاج	tiHtaaj إِنْتَ تِحتاج
walk: 'imshee إمشي	timshee إِنْتَ تِمشي
play: 'ilAeb إلْعَب	tilAeb إِنْتَ تِلْعَب
speak: 'itkellim إتكَلِّم	titkellim إِنْتَ تِتْكَلِّم
give: 'iATee إعْطي	tiATee إِنْتَ تِعْطي
mean: 'iAnee إعني	tiAnee إِنْتَ تِعْني
enjoy: 'itmeteA إتْمَتَع	titmeteA إِنْتَ تِتْمَتَع
read: 'iqraae' تِقْرأ	tiqraae' إِنْتَ تِقْرأ
use: 'isteAmil إسْتَعْمِل	tisteAmil إِنْتَ تِسْتَعْمِل
hear: 'ismeA إسْمَع	tismeA إِنْتَ تِسْمَع
write: 'iktib إكْتِب	tiktib إِنْتَ تِكْتِب
request: 'iTlub إطْلُب	tiTlub إِنْتَ تِطْلُب
sit: 'ijlis إجْلِس	tijlis إِنْتَ تِجْلِس
learn: tAellim تَعَلِّم	titAellim إِنْتَ تِتْعَلِّم
have fun: 'itfeseH إتْفَسَح	titfeseH إِنْتَ تِتْفَسَح
walk: 'imshee إمْشي	timshee إِنْتَ تِمْشي

Spoken Arabic for English Speakers

❷ Learning Step Two: Read aloud to learn the sentence pattern (you + verb + something):

'inte tejeeb ruzz.	إِنْتَ تجيب رُزّ.
'inte tesewwee shaay.	إِنْتَ تَسَوّي شَاي.
'inte tishreb shaay.	إِنْتَ تِشْرَب شَاي.
'inte laa tedrus Hisaab.	إِنْتَ لا تِدْرُس حِساب.
'inte titkellem ketheer.	إِنْتَ تِتْكَلّم كَثير.
'inte terooH lilsooq.	إِنْتَ تروح لِلْسوق.
'inte tejee lilbeyt daa'imen.	إِنْتَ تجي لِلْبَيت دائِماً.
'inte daa'imen tesaafir.	إِنْتَ دائِماً تسافِر.
daa'imen 'inte tezoor 'elmetHef.	دائِماً إِنْتَ تزور أَلْمَتْحَف.
'inte titkellem shweyet Aerebee.	إِنْتَ تِتْكَلّم شْوَيَة عَرَبي.
'inte tereed semek weruzz.	إِنْتَ تريد سَمَك وَرُزّ.
tereed shaay wekeyk kemaan.	تريد شاي وَكَيْك كَمان.
laazim teshoof mekaan kebeer.	لازِم تشوف مَكان كَبير.
helfindiq mish kebeer.	هَلْفِنْدِق مِش كَبير.
tereed mekaan 'ekber mnilfindiq.	تريد مكان أَكْبَر مْنِلْفِنْدِق.
hidhaak findiq kebeer.	هِناك فِنْدِق كَبير.
'inte tejeeb shaay wekeyk.	إِنْتَ تجيب شاي وكَيْك.
tejeeb shaay wekeyk.	تجيب شاي وتجيب كَيْك.
'inte 'illee tejeeb 'ilshaay we'elkeyk.	إِنْتَ إِلّي تجيب أَلْشاي وَأَلْكَيك.
TebAen 'inte 'illee tesewwee 'ilshaay.	طَبْعاً إِنْتَ إِلّي تَسَوّي أَلْشاي.
'eyweh laazim tesewwee 'ilshaay.	أَيْوَه لازِم تَسَوّي أَلْشاي.
'inte tidrus fee 'ilbaalkōon.	إِنْتَ تِدْرُس في أَلْبَالْكون.
'inte teHib tesaafir lidewleh Aerebiyeh.	إِنْتَ تحب تسافِر لِدَوْلَة عَرَبِيَة.
leylaw 'insaaneh muhimeh.	ليلى إِنْسانَة مُهِمَة جِداً.
'inte tiktib kitaab lugheh.	إِنْتَ تِكْتِب كِتاب لُغَة.
'inte teAaal Aindee.	إِنْتَ تِعال عِنْدي.
'inte tereed wereq tiwaaleyt?	إِنْتَ تريد وَرَق تواليت؟
tereed wereq tiwaaleyt?	تريد وَرَق تواليت؟
'inte taakhudh dewa'?	إِنْتَ تاخُذ دَواء؟
taakhudh dewaa'?	تاخُذ دَواء؟
'enaa aakhudh dewaa' sukker.	أَنا آخُذ دَواء سُكَّر.
taakhudh 'esbireen?	تاخُذ أَسْبِرين؟

61

'eyweh aakhudh li'enehu Aindee 'elem.	أَيْوَه آخُذ لِأَنَّه عِنْدي أَلَم؟
laa taakhudh benseleen.	لا تاخُذ بَنْسَلين.
taakul 'ekl mnil shaariA?	تاكُل أكْل منلِشارِع؟
Aindee' feHS 'eydz.	عِنْدي فَحْص أَيْدْز.
leysh treed titAellim Aerebee?	لَيْش تريد تِتْعَلِّم عَرَبي؟
'inte tijlis filmeqhaw ktheer.	إِنْتَ تِجْلِس في أَلْمَقْهى كْثير.
teHib meqhaw 'ilfeeshaawee?	تحب مَقْهى إلْفيشاوي؟
'inte tesaaAid 'ilnaas ktheer.	إِنْتَ تساعَد إلْناس كْثير.
rooH 'itfeseH fee 'ilshaariA.	روح إتْفَسَح في الْشارِع.
'itfeseH fee khaan 'elkheleelee.	إتْفَسَح في خان أَلْخَليلي.
'inte tekoon jemeel lemmeh tiktib.	إِنْتَ تكون جَميل لَمَّه تِكْتِب.
koon kemaa 'inte.	كون كَما أَنْت.

❸ Learning Step Three: Speak aloud with new and old sentence patterns.
❹ Learning Step Four: Write as many sentences as you can remember.

➤Learn these five 5Ws and more:

Who:	meen/minoo	مين
What:	shinoo/shoo/'eyh	شِنو
Where:	weyn/ feyn	وين
When:	me'·taw/ 'imtaw	مَتى
Why:	leysh/leyh	لَيْش
Which:	'ey	أَي
while:	lemmeh	لَمَّه
as:	kemaa	كَما
as in:	kemaa fee	كَما في

meen laylaa?	مين لَيْلى؟
shinoo treed tishreb?	شِنو تُريد تِشْرَب؟
weyn 'ilkitaab?	وِين إلْكِتاب؟
min weyn 'inte?	مِن وَين أَنْتَ؟
'enaa mnil 'iraaq.	أنا مِن أَلْعِراق.
metaw tijee limiSr?	مَتى تَجي لِمِصْر؟
leysh treed tijee limiSr?	لَيْش تُريد تِجي لِمِصْر؟
'ey kitaab tiqraa'?	أَي كِتاب تِقرأ؟

Lesson 7   You (feminine) + Verb إنْتِ تنام

❶ **Learning Step One:** Read aloud to memorize each word's sound and meaning:

you feminine: 'in'·ti	إنْتِ
you want: 'inti teree'·di	إنْتِ تريدِ
Do you want?: 'inte tereedi?	إنْتِ تريدِ؟
you bring: 'inti tejee'·bi	إنْتِ تجيبِ
you sleep: 'inti tenee'·mi	إنْتِ تنامِ
you see: 'inti teshoo'·fi	إنْتِ تشوفِ
you buy: 'inti tish'·ti·ri	إنْتِ تِشتِرِ
you walk: 'inti tim'·shi	إنْتِ تِمْشِ
be (feminine): koo'·nee	كوني
you (feminine) become: 'inti tekoo'·ni	إنْتِ تكونِ
friend: Se·deeq'	صَديق
friend (feminine): Se·dee'·qeh	صَديقَة
friends: 'eS·di·qaa'	أَصْدِقاء
verb: fiAl	فِعْل
do: 'if'·Ael	إفْعَل
do (feminine): 'if'·Ae·li	إفْعَلِ

Verb Conjugations

We usually add the prefix (te تَ) to conjugate a verb from a command form as in (shoof شوف) to ('inti teshoofi تشوفِ إنْتِ), and we add the short vowel kesreh "i" at the end of the verb. So, teshoof becomes teshoofi.

<u>command form verb</u>   <u>she + verb</u>

command form verb		she + verb	
bring: jeeb	جيب	tejeebi	إنْتِ تجيبِ
sleep: naam	نام	tenaami	إنْتِ تنامِ
see: shoof	شوف	teshoofi	إنْتِ تشوفِ
get up: qoom	قوم	teqoomi	إنْتِ تقومِ
go: rooH	روح	terooHi	إنْتِ تروحِ
put: HuT	حُطّ	teHuti	إنْتِ تحُطِ

love: Hib حِب	إنْتِ تحِب teHibi
feel: Hiss حِس	إنْتِ تحِس teHisi
think: fekir فَكِر	إنْتِ تفَكِر tefekiri
cut: qeTiA قَطِع	إنْتِ تقَطِع teqeTiAi
thaw: dhewwib ذَوِّب	إنْتِ تذَوِّبِ tedhewwibi
do/make: sewwee سَوِّي	إنْتِ تسَوِّي tesewwee
come: teAaal/jee تَعال/ جي	إنْتِ تجي tejee
study: 'udrus أدرُس	إنْتِ تدرُس tedrusi
help: saaAid ساعِد	إنْتِ تساعِد tesaaAidi
be: koon كون	إنْتِ تكون tekooni
eat: kul كُل	إنْتِ تاكُلِ taakuli
take: khudh خُذ	إنْتِ تاخُذِ taakhudhi
take/grab: haak هاك	هاكي haakee

➤ As in 'ishreb إشْرَب, when the verb in a command form begins with ('i إ) the ('i إ) is not silent and it stays when conjugated to (you (f) drink: tishrebi إنْتِ تِشرَب):

drink: 'ishreb إشْرَب	إنْتِ تِشرَبِ tishrebi
work: 'ishtughul إشتُغُل	إنْتِ تِشْتَغِل tishtegheli
buy: 'ishteree إشتَرِي	إنْتِ تِشتَرِي tishteree
talk: 'iHkee إحْكِي	إنْتِ تحكِي tiHkee
need: 'iHtaaj إحْتَاج	إنْتِ تِحْتَاج tiHtaaji
walk: 'imshee إمْشِي	إنْتِ تِمْشِي timshee
play: 'ilAeb إلْعَب	إنْتِ تِلْعَبِ tilAebi
speak: 'itkellim إتكَلِّم	إنْتِ تِتْكَلِّمِ titkellimi
give: 'iATee إعْطِي	إنْتِ تِعْطِي tiATee
mean: 'iAnee إعْنِي	إنْتِ تِعْنِي tiAnee
enjoy: 'itmeteA إتْمَتَع	إنْتِ تِتمَتَعِ titmeteAi
read: 'iqraae' تِقْرأ	إنْتِ تِقْرأي tiqraae'ee
use: 'isteAmil إسْتَعْمِل	إنْتِ تِسْتَعْمِلِ tisteAmili
hear: 'ismeA إسْمَع	إنْتِ تِسْمَعِ tismeAi
write: 'iktib إكْتِب	إنْتِ تكتِبِ tiktibi
request: 'iTlub إطْلُب	إنْتِ تِطْلُبِ tiTlubi
sit: 'ijlis إجْلِس	إنْتِ تِجْلِسِ tijlisi

learn: tAellim تُعَلِّم   titAellimi إِنْتِ تِتْعَلِّمِ

have fun: 'itfeseH إِتْفَسَح   titfeseHi إِنْتِ تِتْفَسَحِ

❷ Learning Step Two: Read aloud to learn the sentence pattern (you (f.) + verb + something):

'inti tejeebi ruzz. إِنْتِ تجيبِ رُزّ.

'inti tesewwee shaay. إِنْتِ تسَوّي شاي.

'inti tishrebi shaay. إِنْتِ تِشْرَبِ شاي.

'inti laa tedrusi Hisaab. إِنْتِ لا تِدْرُسِ حِساب.

'inti titkellemi ketheer. إِنْتِ تِتْكَلَّمِ كَثير.

'inti terooHi lilsooq. إِنْتِ تروحِ لِلْسوق.

'inti tejee lilbeyt daa'imen. إِنْتِ تجي لِلْبَيت دائِماً.

'inti daa'imen tesaafiri. إِنْتِ دائِماً تسافِرِ.

daa'imen 'inti tezoori 'elmetHef. دائِماً إِنْتِ تزورِ أَلْمَتْحَف.

'inti titkellemi shweyet Aerebee. إِنْتِ تِتْكَلَّمِ شْوَيَة عَرَبي.

'inti tereedi semek weruzz. إِنْتِ تريدِ سَمَك وَرُزّ.

tereedi shaay wekeyk kemaan. تريدِ شاي وَكَيْك كَمان.

laazim teshoofi mekaan kebeer. لازم تشوفِ مَكان كَبير.

'inti tejeebi shaay wekeyk. إِنْتِ تجيبِ شاي وكَيْك.

tejeebi shaay wekeyk. تجيبِ شاي وتجيبِ كَيْك.

'inti 'illee tejeebi 'ilshaay we'elkeyk. إِنْتِ إِلّي تجيبِ أَلْشاي وَأَلْكَيك.

TebAen 'inti 'illee tesewwee 'ilshaay. طَبْعاً إِنْتِ إِلّي تسَوّي أَلْشاي.

'eyweh laazim tesewwee 'ilshaay. أَيْوَه لازم تسَوّي أَلْشاي.

'inti tidrusi fee 'ilbaalkoon. إِنْتِ تِدرُس في أَلْبالْكون.

'inti teHibi tesaafiri lidewleh Aerebiyeh. إِنْتِ تحبِ تسافِرِ لِدَولَة عَرَبِيَة.

leylaw Sedeeqeh muhimeh. ليلى صَديقَة مُهِمَة جِداً.

'inti tiktibi kitaab lugheh. إِنْتِ تِكْتِبِ كِتاب لُغَة.

'inti teAaali Aindee. إِنْتِ تِعالِ عِنْدي.

'inti tereedi wereq tiwaaleyt? إِنْتِ تريدِ وَرَق تِواليت؟

tereedi wereq tiwaaleyt? تريدِ وَرَق تِواليت؟

'inti taakhudhi dewa'? إِنْتِ تاخِذِ دَواء؟

taakhudhi 'esbireen? تاخِذِ أَسْبِرين؟

laa taakhudhi benseleen. لا تاخِذِ بَنْسَلين.

taakuli 'ekl mnil shaariA? تاكلِ أَكْل مِنِلْشارِع؟

leysh treedi titAellim Aerebee?	لَيْش تريد تِتْعَلّم عَرَبي؟
'inti tijlisi filmeqhaw ktheer.	إِنْتِ تِجْلِس في أَلْمَقْهى كثير.
teHibi meqhaw 'ilfeeshaawee?	تحب مَقْهى إِلْفيشاوي؟
'inti tesaaAidi 'ilnaas ktheer.	إِنْتِ تساعَد إِلْناس كُثير.
rooHi 'itfeseHi fee 'ilshaariA.	روح إِتْفَسَح في إِلْشارِع.
'itfeseHi fee khaan 'elkheleelee.	إِتْفَسَح في خان أَلْخَليلي.
'inti tekooni jemeeleh lemmeh tiktibi.	إِنْتِ تكون جَميلَة لَمَّه تِكْتِب.
kem (how many) Sadeeqeh Aindik?	كَم صَديقَة عِنْدِك؟
Aindik 'eSdiqaa' ketheer?	عِنْدِك أَصْدِقاء كثير؟

❸ Learning Step Three: Speak aloud with new and old sentence patterns.
❹ Learning Step Four: Write as many sentences as you can remember.

Lesson 8   هُم ينامون   They + Verb

Spoken Arabic for English Speakers

❶ Learning Step One: Read aloud to memorize each word's sound and meaning:

they: hum	هُم
they want: hum y*e*ree′·doon	هُم يريدون
they don't want: hum laa y*e*reedoon	هُم لا يريدون
they speak: hum yi·tekel·li·moon′	هُم بِتْكَلِّمون
go down/get off: 'in′·zil	إِنْزِل
they get off: hum y*e*nziloon	هُم ينزلون
friends: 'eS·di·qaa'	أَصْدِقاء
relatives: 'e·qaa′·rib	أَقارِب
eSdiqaa we'eqaarib yijoon	أَصْدِقاء وأَقارِب يِجون

Verb Conjugations

command form verb	they + verb
bring: jeeb جيب	y*e*jeeboon هُم يجيبون
sleep: naam نام	y*e*naamoon هُم ينامون
see: shoof شوف	y*e*shoofoon هُم يشوفون
get up: qoom قوم	y*e*qoomoon هُم يقومون
go: rooH روح	y*e*rooHoon هُم يروحون
put: HuT حُط	y*e*Hutoon هُم يحطون
love: Hib حِب	y*e*Hiboon هُم يحِبون
feel: Hiss حِس	y*e*Hisoon هُم يحِسون
think: fekir فَكِر	y*e*fekiroon هُم يفَكِرون
cut: qeTiA قَطِع	y*e*qeTiAoon هُم يقَطِعون
thaw: dhewwib ذَوِّب	y*e*dhewwiboon هُم يذَوِّبون
do/make: sewwee سَوّي	y*e*sewwoon هُم يسَوّون
come: teAaal/jee تَعال/ جي	y*e*joon هُم يجون
study: 'udrus أُدْرُس	y*e*drisoon هُم بِدرُسون
eat: kul كُل	yaakuloon هُم ياكُلون
take: khudh خُذ	yaakhudhoon هُم ياخُذون

help: saaAid ساعِد	هُم يساعدون yesaaAidoon
be: koon كون	هُم يكونون yekoonoon

➤ As in 'ishreb إشْرَب, when the verb in a command form begins with ('i إ) the ('i إ) is not silent and it stays when conjugated to (they drink: yishreboon هُم يِشرَبون):

drink: 'ishreb إشْرَب	yishreboon هُم يِشرَبون
work: 'ishteghul إشْتَغُل	yishtugheloon هُم يِشْتَغُلون
buy: 'ishteree إشْتِري	yishteroon هُم يِشْتِرون
talk: 'iHkee إحْكي	yiHkoon هُم يِحكون
need: 'iHtaaj إحْتاج	yiHtaajoon هُم يِحْتاجون
walk: 'imshee إمْشي	yimshoon هُم يِمْشون
play: 'ilAeb إلْعَب	yilAeboon هُم يِلْعَبون
speak: 'itkellim إتكَلِّم	yitkellimoon هُم يِتْكَلِّمون
give: 'iATee إعْطي	yiAToon هُم يِعْطون
mean: 'iAnee إعْني	yiAnoon هُم يِعْنون
enjoy: 'itmeteA إتْمَتَع	yitmeteAoon هُم يِتْمَتَعون
read: 'iqraae' إقْرَأ	yiqraae'oon هُم يِقْرَأون
use: 'isteAmil إسْتَعْمِل	yisteAmiloon هُم يِسْتَعْمِلون
hear: 'ismeA إسْمَع	yismeAoon هُم يِسْمَعون
write: 'iktib إكْتِب	yiktiboon هُم يِكْتِبون
request/ask for: 'iTlub إطْلُب	yiTluboon هُم يِطْلُبون
sit: 'ijlis إجْلِس	yijlisoon هُم يِجْلِسون
learn: tAellim تْعَلِّم	yitAellimoon هُم يِتْعَلِّمون
have fun: 'itfeseH إتْفَسَح	yitfeseHoon هُم يِتْفَسَحون

❷ Learning Step Two: Read aloud to learn the sentence pattern (they + verb + something):

hum yejeeboon ruzz.	هُم يجيبون رُزّ.
hum yesewwoon shaay.	هُم يسوّون شاي.
hum yishreboon shaay.	هُم يِشْرَبون شاي.
hum laa yedrusoon Hisaab.	هُم لا يِدْرسون حِساب.
hum yitkellemoom ketheer.	هُم يِتْكَلِّمون كَثير.
hum yerooHoon lilsooq.	هُم يروحون لِلسوق.
hum yejoon lilbeyt daa'imen.	هُم يجون لِلبَيت دائماً.

hum daa'imen yesaafiroon.	هُم دائِماً يسافِرونِ.
daa'imen hum yezooroon 'elmetHef.	دائِماً هُم يزورونِ أَلْمَتْحَفِ.
hum yitkellemoon shweyet Aerebee.	هُم بِتْكَلِّمون شْوَيَة عَرَبي.
hum yereedoon semek weruzz.	هُم يريدون سَمَك وَرُزّ.
yereedi shaay wekeyk kemaan.	يريدون شاي وَكَيْك كَمان.
laazim yeshoofoon mekaan kebeer.	لازم يشوفون مَكان گبير.
hum yejeeboon shaay wekeyk.	هُم يجيبون شاي وكَيْك.
yejeebi shaay wekeyk.	يجيبون شاي وكَيْك.
hum 'illee yejeeboon 'elkeyk.	هُم إِلْلي يجيبون أَلْكَيك.
hum 'illee yesewwoon 'ilshaay.	هُم إِلْلي يسَوّون أَلْشاي.
laazim yesewwoon 'ilshaay.	لازم يسَوّون أَلْشاي.
hum yedrusoon fee 'ilbaalkōon.	هُم يدرُسون في أَلْبالْكون.
hum yeHiboon yesaafiroon.	هُم يحبون يسافرون.
hum yektiboon kitaab lugheh.	هُم يكْتِبون كِتاب لُغَة.
hum yereedoon wereq tiwaaleyt?	هُم يريدون وَرَق تِواليت؟
yereedoon wereq tiwaaleyt?	يريدون وَرَق تِواليت؟
hum yaakhudhoon dewa'?	هُم ياخذون دَواء؟
leysh yaakuloon 'ekl mnil shaariA?	ليش ياكلون أَكْل مِنِلْشارِع؟
leysh yreedoon yitAellimoon Aerebee?	لَيْش يريدون يتْعَلِّمون عَرَبي؟
hum yijlisoon filmeqhaw ktheer.	هُم يجلسون في أَلْمَقْهى كثير.
yeHiboon meqhaw 'ilfeeshaawee?	يحبون مَقْهى إِلْفيشاوي؟
hum yesaaAidoon 'ilnaas ktheer.	هُم يساعْدون إِلْناس كْثير.
yitfeseHoon fee khaan 'elkheleelee.	بِتْفَسَحّون في خان أَلْخَليلي.

❸ Learning Step Three: Speak aloud with new and old sentence patterns.
❹ Learning Step Four: Write as many sentences as you can remember.

Lesson 9 — You (plural) sleep إنْتو تَنامون

❶ Learning Step One: Read aloud to memorize each word's sound and meaning:

you (plural): 'in·too'	إنْتو
you (p.) sleep: 'intoo tenaa'·moon	إنْتو تنامون
you (p.) bring: 'intoo tejee'·boon	إنْتو تجيبون
you (p.) want: 'intoo teree'·doon	إنْتو تريدون
you (p.) want: teree'·doon	تريدون
you (p.) speak: 'intoo ti·tekel·li·moon'	إنْتو تِتْكَلِّمون
you (p.) get off: 'intoo tenzi·loon'	إنْتو تنزلون
you (p.) say: 'intoo teqee'·loon	إنْتو تقولون
you (p.) be: 'intoo tekoo'·noon	إنْتو تكونون
you (p.) become: 'intoo teSee'·roon	إنْتو تصيرون
you (p.) are friends: 'intoo 'eS·di·qaa'	إنْتو أصْدِقاء
you (p.) are relatives: 'intoo 'e·qaa'·rib	إنْتو أقارِب
a thing: shee	شي

Verb Conjugations

command form verb	you plural + verb
bring: jeeb جيب	tejeeboon إنْتو تجيبون
sleep: naam نام	tenaamoon إنْتو تنامون
see: shoof شوف	teshoofoon إنْتو تشوفون
get up: qoom قوم	teqoomoon إنْتو تقومون
go: rooH روح	terooHoon إنْتو تروحون
put: HuT حُط	teHutoon إنْتو تحطون
love: Hib حِب	teHiboon إنْتو تحبون
feel: Hiss حِس	teHisoon إنْتو تحسون
think: fekir فَكِر	tefekiroon إنْتو تفكرون
cut: qeTiA قَطِع	teqeTiAoon إنْتو تقطعون
thaw: dhewwib ذَوِّب	tedhewwiboon إنْتو تذَوِّبون
do/make: sewwee سَوّي	tesewwoon إنْتو تسَوّون

come: teAaal/jee تَعال/ جي	إنْتو تجون tejoon
study: 'udrus أدْرُس	إنْتو تدرسون tedrisoon
eat: kul كُل	إنْتو تاكُلون taakuloon
take: khudh خُذ	إنْتو تاخُذون taakhudhoon
help: saaAid ساعِد	إنْتو تساعدون tesaaAidoon
be: koon كون	إنْتو تكونون tekoonoon

➤ As in 'ishreb إشْرَب, when the verb in a command form begins with ('i إ) the ('i إ) is not silent and it stays when conjugated to (you (plural) drink: tishreboon إنْتو تِشْرَبون):

drink: 'ishreb إشْرَب	إنْتو تِشرَبون tishreboon
work: 'ishteghul إشتُغُل	إنْتو تِشْتَغُلون tishtughloon
buy: 'ishteree إشتَري	إنْتو تِشتَرون tishteroon
talk: 'iHkee إحْكي	إنْتو تِحكون tiHkoon
need: 'iHtaaj إحْتاج	إنْتو تِحْتاجون tiHtaajoon
walk: 'imshee إمْشي	إنْتو تِمْشون timshoon
play: 'ilAeb إلْعَب	إنْتو تِلْعَبون tilAeboon
speak: 'itkellim إتكَلَّم	إنْتو تِتْكَلَّمون titkellimoon
give: 'iATee إعْطي	إنْتو تِعْطون tiAToon
mean: 'iAnee إعني	إنْتو تِعْنون tiAnoon
enjoy: 'itmeteA إتْمَتَع	إنْتو تِتمَتَعون tetmeteAoon
read: 'iqraae' إقْرأ	إنْتو تِقْرأون tiqraae'oon
use: 'isteAmil إسْتَعْمِل	إنْتو تِسْتَعْمِلون tisteAmiloon
hear: 'ismeA إسْمَع	إنْتو تِسْمَعون tismeAoon
write: 'iktib إكْتِب	إنْتو تِكْتِبون tiktiboon
request/ask for: 'iTlub إطْلُب	إنْتو تِطْلُبون tiTluboon
sit: 'ijlis إجْلِس	إنْتو تِجْلِسون tijlisoon
learn: tAellim تْعَلِّم	إنْتو تِتْعَلِّمون titAellimoon
have fun: 'itfeseH إتْفَسَح	إنْتو تِتْفَسَحون titfeseHoon

❷ Learning Step Two: Read aloud to learn the sentence pattern (they + verb + something):

'intoo tejeeboon ruzz.	إنْتو تجيبون رُزّ.
'intoo tesewwoon shaay.	إنْتو تسَوّون شاي.
'intoo tishreboon shaay.	إنْتو تِشْرَبون شاي.
'intoo laa tedrusoon Hisaab.	إنْتو لا تدرسون حِساب.

'intoo titkellemoom ketheer.	إِنْتو تِتْكَلِّمون كثير.
'intoo terooHoon lilsooq.	إِنْتو تروحون لِلْسوق.
'intoo tijoon lilbett daa'imen.	إِنْتو تِجون لِلْبَيت دائِماً.
'intoo daa'imen tesaafiroon.	إِنْتو دائِماً تسافِرون.
daa'imen tezooroon 'elmetHef.	دائِماً تزورون أَلْمَتْحَف.
'intoo titkellemoon Aerebee?	إِنْتو تِتْكَلِّمون عَرَبي؟
'intoo tereedoon semek weruzz?	إِنْتو تريدون سَمَك وَرُزّ؟
tereedi shaay wekeyk kemaan?	تِريدون شاي وَكَيْك كَمان؟
laazim teshoofoon mekaan kebeer.	لازِم تشوفون مَكان كبير.
'intoo tejeeboon shaay wekeyk.	إِنْتو تجيبون شاي وكَيْك.
'intoo 'illee tejeeboon 'elkeyk.	إِنْتو إِلْي تجيبون أَلْكَيك.
'intoo 'illee tesewwoon 'ilshaay.	إِنْتو إِلْي تسَوّون أَلْشاي.
laazim tesewwoon 'ilshaay.	لازِم تسَوّون أَلْشاي.
'intoo tedrusoon fee 'ilbaalkōon.	إِنْتو تدرُسون في أَلْبالْكون.
'intoo teHiboon tesaafiroon.	إِنْتو تحبون تسافِرون.
'intoo tektiboon kitaab lugheh.	إِنْتو تكْتِبون كِتاب لُغَة.
'intoo tereedoon wereq tiwaalett?	إِنْتو تريدون وَرَق تِواليت؟
'intoo taakhudhoon dewa'?	إِنْتو تاخذون دَواء؟
letsh taakuloon 'ekl mnil shaariA?	ليش تاكلون أَكْل منِلشارع؟
letsh treedoon titAellimoon Aerebee?	لَيْش تريدون تتْعَلّمون عَرَبي؟
'intoo tijlisoon filmeqhaw ktheer.	إِنْتو تجلسون في أَلْمَقْهى كثير.
teHiboon meqhaw 'ilfeeshaawee?	تحبون مَقْهى إِلْفيشاوي؟
'intoo tesaaAidoon 'ilnaas ktheer.	إِنْتو تساعْدون إِلْناس كُثير.
titfeseHoon fee khaan 'elkheleelee.	تِتْفَسَحون في خان أَلْخَليلي.
'intoo tinziloon mnil Taa'reh.	إِنْتو تِنزِلون مِن أَلْطائِرَة.
inziloo fee findiq qereeb.	إِنْزِلوا في فِنْدِق قَريب.
teHtaajoon shee?	تحتاجون شي؟
'intoo tekoo'·noon meAi	إِنْتو تكونون مَعي.
iboon tesaafiroon meAi?	تحبون تسافرون مَعي؟

❸ Learning Step Three: Speak aloud with new and old sentence patterns.
❹ Learning Step Four: Write as many sentences as you can remember.

Lesson 10 — Future Tense Verbs: He'll sleep هو راح يَنام

❶ Learning Step One: Read aloud to memorize these word's sound and meaning:

will: raaH	راح
I will go: raaH 'e·rooH'	أنا راح أروح
He will go: raaH yerooH	هُوَ راح يروح
She will go: raaH terooH	هِيَ راح تروح
You will go: raaH terooH	إنْتَ راح تروح
You (f) will go: raaH teroo'·Hi	إنْتِ راح تروحِ
We will go: raaH nerooH	نَحْنُ راح نروح
They will go: raaH yeroo'·Hoon	هُم راح يروحون
You (plural) will go: 'entoo raaH teroo'·Hoon	إنْتو راح تروحون

❷ Learning Step Two: Read aloud to learn the sentence pattern (someone will + verb + something):

'enaa raaH 'ejeeb ruzz.	أنا راح أجيب رُزّ.
'enaa raaH 'esewwee shaay.	أنا راح أسَوّي شاي.
'enaa raaH 'eshreb shaay.	أنا راح أشْرَب شاي.
'enaa raaH 'erooH lilsooq.	أنا راح أروح لِلْسوق.
raaH 'ejee lilbeyt.	راح أجي لِلْبَيت.
daa'imen raaH 'esaafir.	دائِماً راح أسافِر.
daa'imen raaH 'ezoor 'elmetHef.	دائِماً راح أزور ألْمَتْحَف.
raaH 'eshoof mekaan kebeer.	راح أشوف مَكان كَبير.
raaH 'ejeeb shaay wekeyk.	راح أجيب شاي وكَيْك.
raaH 'ejeeb shaay wekeyk.	أجيب شاي وأجيب كَيْك.
'enaa 'illee raaH 'ejeeb elkeyk.	أنا إلْلي راح أجيب ألْكَيك.
daa'men raaH 'ejeeb keyk.	دائِماً أجيب كَيك.
'enaa 'illee raaH 'esewwee 'ilshaay.	أنا إلْلي راح أسَوّي ألْشاي.
huwe raaH raaH yejeeb ruzz.	هُوَ راح يجيب رُزّ.
huwe raaH yesewwee shaay.	هُوَ راح يسَوّي شاي.
huwe raaH yeshreb shaay.	هُوَ راح بِشْرَب شاي.
huwe raaH yerooH lilsooq.	هُوَ راح يروح لِلْسوق.

raaH y*e*jee lilbeyt.	راح يجي لِلْبَيت.
huwe raaH y*e*saafir daa'imen.	هُوَ راح يسافِر دائِماً.
huwe raaH y*e*zoor 'elmetHef.	هُوَ راح يزور أَلْمَتْحَف.
raaH y*e*tkellem Aerebee.	راح بِتْكَلِّم عَرَبي.
raaH y*e*shoof mekaan kebeer.	راح يشوف مَكان كَبير.
huwe raaH y*e*jeeb keyk.	هُوَ راح يجيب كَيْك.
raaH y*e*jeeb shaay wekeyk.	راح يجيب شاي وكَيْك.
raaH y*e*sewwee 'ilshaay.	راح يسَوّي أَلْشاي.
raaH y*e*tkellem Aerebee.	راح بِتكَلِّم عَرَبي.
aadem raaH y*e*drus fee miSr.	آدَم راح يدرُس في مَصر.
saam raaH yishteghil muweZef.	سام راح بِشْتَغِل مُوَظَف.
jaak raaH y*e*Tbukh 'ekl ledheedh	جاك راح يطبُخ أَكُل لَذيذ.
joorj raaH y*aa*kul 'ekl Aerebee	جورج راح ياكُل أَكُل عَرَبي.
'ilmuAellim raaH y*e*Seer mumethil.	إِلْمُعَلِّم راح يصير مُمَثِل.
neHnu raaH n*e*jeeb ruzz.	نَحْنُ راح نجيب رُزّ.
neHnu raaH n*e*sewwee shaay.	نَحْنُ راح نسَوّي شاي.
raaH nishreb shaay.	راح نِشْرَب شاي.
raaH n*e*drus Hisaab.	راح ندْرُس حِساب.
neHnu raaH nitkellem ketheer.	نَحْنُ راح نِتْكَلِّم كَثير.
neHnu raaH n*e*rooH lilsooq.	نَحْنُ راح نروح لِلْسوق.
raaH n*e*jee lilbeyt.	راح نجي لِلْبَيت.
neHnu raaH daa'imen n*e*saafir.	نَحْنُ راح دائِماً نسافِر.
daa'imen raaH n*e*zoor 'elmetHef.	دائِماً راح نزور أَلْمَتْحَف.
raaH nitkellem Aerebee.	راح نِتكَلِّم عَرَبي.
raaH n*e*shoof mekaan kebeer.	راح نشوف مَكان كَبير.
neHnu 'illee raaH n*e*jeeb'elkeyk.	نَحْنُ إِلّي راح نجيب أَلْكَيك.
raaH n*e*sewwee 'ilshaay.	راح نسَوّي أَلْشاي.
raaH nitkellem Aerebee.	راح نِتكَلِّم عَرَبي.
'enaa weaadem raaH n*e*drus.	أَنا وآدَم راح ندرُس.
raaH n*e*shoof 'ilHraam.	راح نشوف الأَهْرام.
'enaa wejemaal n*e*jeeb mey.	أَنا وجمال راح نجيب مَي.

raaH nishteghil.	راح نِشتِغِل.
raaH naakul beyD.	راح ناكُل بَيْض.
raaH nitkillim Aerebee	راح نِتْكَلِّم عَرَبي.
neHnu raaH neTbukh.	نَحْنُ راح نطبُخ.
hiye raaH tejeeb ruzz.	هِيَ راح تجيب رُزّ.
hiye raaH tesewwee shaay.	هِيَ راح تسَوّي شاي.
hiye raaH tishreb shaay.	هِيَ راح تِشْرَب شاي.
hiye raaH tedrus Hisaab.	هِيَ راح تِدْرُس حِساب.
hiye raaH titkellem ketheer.	هِيَ راح تِتْكَلِّم كَثير.
hiye raaH terooH lilsooq.	هِيَ راح تروح لِلْسوق.
hiye raaH tejee lilbeyt daa'imen.	هِيَ راح تجي لِلْبَيت دائِماً.
hiye raaH daa'imen tesaafir.	هِيَ راح دائِماً تِسافِر.
hiye raaH titkellem Aerebee.	هِيَ راح تِتْكَلِّم عَرَبي.
raaH teshoof mekaan kebeer.	لازِم تشوف مَكان كَبير.
hiye raaH tejeeb keyk.	هِيَ راح تجيب كَيْك.
hiye 'illee raaH tesewwee 'ilshaay.	هِيَ إلّي راح تسَوّي ألْشاي.
naadiyaa raaH tidrus fee 'ilbaalkōon.	نادِيا تِدْرُس في ألْبالْكون.
jemeeleh raaH tilbes fustaan jemeel.	جَميلة راح تِلْبَس فُستان جَميل.
hiye raaH tesaafir lidewleh Aerebiyeh.	هِيَ راح تسافِر لِدَولَة عَرَبِيَة.
raaH tiktib kitaab lugheh Aerebiyeh.	راح تِكْتِب كِتاب لُغَة عَرَبِيَة.
'inte raaH tejeeb ruzz.	إنْتَ راح تجيب رُزّ.
'inte raaH tesewwee shaay.	إنْتَ راح تسَوّي شاي.
'inte raaH tishreb shaay.	إنْتَ راح تِشْرَب شاي.
'inte raaH laa tedrus Hisaab.	إنْتَ راح لا تِدْرُس حِساب.
'inte raaH titkellem ketheer.	إنْتَ راح تِتْكَلِّم كَثير.
'inte raaH terooH lilsooq.	إنْتَ راح تروح لِلْسوق.
'inte raaH tejee lilbeyt daa'imen.	إنْتَ راح تجي لِلْبَيت دائِماً.
'inte raaH daa'imen tesaafir.	إنْتَ راح دائِماً تِسافِر.
raaH terooH lilmetHef.	راح تروح لِلْمَتْحَف.
raaH titkellem Aerebee.	راح تِتْكَلِّم عَرَبي.

teshoof mekaan kebeer.	راح تشوف مَكان كَبير.
'inte 'illee raaH tejeeb 'elkeyk.	إنْتَ إلّي راح تجيب ألْكَيك.
'inte 'illee raaH tesewwee 'ilshaay.	إنْتَ إلّي راح تسَوّي ألْشاي.
raaH tidrus fee 'ilbaalkōon?	راح تِدرُس في ألْبالْكون؟
raaH tijee Aindee?	راح تِجي عِنْدي؟
raaH tiktib kitaab.	راح تِكْتِب كِتاب.
meen raaH tiktib?	مين راح تِكْتِب كِتاب؟
'inte raaH tiktib 'ew hiye raaH tiktib?	إنْتَ راح تِكْتِب أو هِيَ راح تِكْتِب؟
'inte raaH taakhudh dewa'?	إنْتَ راح تاخُذ دَواء؟
raaH aakhudh dewaa' sukker.	راح آخُذ دَواء سُكَّر.
raaH taakul 'ekl mnil shaariA?	راح تاكُل أكْل منِلشارِع؟
lesh raaH titAellim Aerebee?	لَيْش راح تِتْعَلِّم عَرَبي؟
'inte raaH tesaaAid 'ilnaas ktheer.	إنْتَ راح تساعَد إلْناس كْثير.
raaH tekoon kemaa 'inte.	راح تكون كَما أنْت.
'inti raaH raaH tejeebi ruzz.	إنْتِ راح تجيبِ رُزّ.
'inti raaH tesewwee shaay.	إنْتِ راح تسَوّي شاي.
'inti raaH tishrebi shaay.	إنْتِ راح تِشْرَبِ شاي.
'inti raaH laa tedrusi Hisaab.	إنْتِ راح لا تِدْرُس حِساب.
'inti raaH titkellemi ketheer.	إنْتِ راح تِتْكَلِّم كَثير.
'inti raaH terooHi lilsooq.	إنْتِ راح تروح لِلْسوق.
'inti raaH tejee lilbeyt daa'imen.	إنْتِ راح تجي لِلْبَيت دائِماً.
'inti raaH daa'imen tesaafiri.	إنْتِ راح دائِماً تسافِر.
'inti raaH titkellemi Aerebee.	إنْتِ راح تِتْكَلِّم عَرَبي.
raaH teshoofi mekaan kebeer.	راح تشوفِ مَكان كَبير.
'inti raaH tejeebi keyk.	إنْتِ راح تجيب كَيْك.
mish 'inti 'illee raaH tejeebi 'elkeyk.	مِش إنْتِ إلّي راح تجيب ألْكَيك.
'inti 'illee raaH tesewwee 'ilshaay.	إنْتِ إلّي راح تسَوّي ألْشاي.
raaH tidrusi fee 'ilbaalkoon?	راح تِدرُسِ في ألْبالْكون؟
raaH tiktibi kitaab?	راح تِكْتِب كِتاب؟
raaH tejee Aindee?	راح تِجي عِنْدي؟
raaH taakhudhi 'esbireen?	راح تاخُذِ أسْبِرين؟

raaH taak*u*li 'ekl mnil shaariA?	راح تاكلِ أُكْل منِلشارع؟
raaH tijlisi filmeqhaw ktheer?	راح تِجْلِس في أَلْمَقْهى كثير؟
raaH t*e*Hibi meqhaw 'ilfeeshaawee?	راح تحبِ مَقْهى إِلْفيشاوي؟
'inti raaH t*e*saaAidi 'ilnaas ktheer.	إِنْتِ راح تساعَدِ إِلْناس كْثير.

hum raaH y*e*jeeboon ruzz.	هُم راح يجيبون رُزّ.
hum raaH y*e*sewwoon shaay.	هُم راح يسَوّون شاي.
hum raaH yishreboon shaay.	هُم راح بِشْرَبون شاي.
hum raaH yitkellemoom ktheer.	هُم راح بِتْكَلِّمون كَثير.
hum raaH y*e*rooHoon lilsooq.	هُم راح يروحون لِلْسوق.
hum raaH y*e*joon lilbeyt daa'imen.	هُم راح يجون لِلْبَيت دائِماً.
hum raaH daa'imen y*e*saafiroon.	هُم راح دائِماً يسافِرون.
hum raaH yitkellemoon Aerebee.	هُم راح بِتْكَلِّمون عَرَبي.
raaH y*e*shoofoon mekaan kebeer.	راح يشوفون مَكان كَبير.
hum raaH y*e*jeeboon keyk.	هُم راح يجيبون كَيْك.
hum 'illee raaH y*e*jeeboon 'elkeyk.	هُم إِلّي راح يجيبون أَلْكَيك.
hum raaH y*e*sewwoon 'ilshaay.	هُم راح يسَوّون أَلْشاي.
'ekeed raaH y*e*sewwoon 'ilshaay.	أَكيد راح يسَوّون أَلْشاي.
raaH y*e*drusoon fee 'ilbaalkōon.	راح يدرُسون في أَلْبالْكون.
raaH y*e*Hiboon y*e*saafiroon.	راح يحبون يسافرون.
raaH y*e*ktiboon kitaab.	راح يكْتِبون كِتاب.
raaH yaakh*u*dhoon dewa'.	راح ياخذون دَواء.
leysh yaak*u*loon mnil shaariA?	ليش راح ياكلون منِلشارع؟
leysh raaH yitAellimoon Aerebee?	لَيْش راح يتْعَلِّمون عَرَبي؟
raaH yijlisoon filmeqhaw ktheer.	راح يجلسون في أَلْمَقْهى كثير.
hum raaH y*e*saaAidoon 'ilnaas.	هُم راح يساعْدون إِلْناس.
raaH yitfeseHoon kemaan.	راح بِتْفَسَحون كمان.
raaH y*e*Seeroon 'eSdiqaa',	راح يصيرون أَصْدِقاء.
mish raaH yiHtaajoon shee.	مِش راح بِحتاجون شي.

'intoo raaH t*e*jeeboon ruzz.	إِنْتو راح تجيبون رُزّ.
'intoo raaH t*e*sewwoon shaay.	إِنْتو راح تسَوّون شاي.

'intoo raaH tishreboon shaay.	إِنْتو راح تِشْرَبون شاي.
'intoo raaH titkellemoom ketheer.	إِنْتو راح تِتْكَلِّمون كَثير.
'intoo raaH terooHoon lilsooq.	إِنْتو راح تروحون لِلْسوق.
'intoo raaH tejoon lilbeyt daa'imen.	إِنْتو راح تجون لِلْبَيت دائِماً.
'intoo raaH daa'imen tesaafiroon.	إِنْتو راح دائِماً تسافرون.
'intoo raaH titkellemoon Aerebee.	إِنْتو راح تِتْكَلِّمون عَرَبي.
raaH teshoofoon mekaan kebeer.	راح تشوفون مَكان كَبير.
'intoo raaH tejeeboon keyk.	إِنْتو راح تجيبون كَيْك.
'intoo 'illee raaH tejeeboon 'elkeyk.	إِنْتو إِلّي راح تجيبون أَلْكَيك.
'intoo raaH tesewwoon 'ilshaay.	إِنْتو راح تسَوّون أَلْشاي.
'ekeed raaH tesewwoon 'ilshaay.	أَكيد راح تسَوّون أَلْشاي.
raaH tedrusoon fee 'ilbaalkōon.	راح تدرُسون في أَلْبالْكون.
raaH teHiboon tesaafiroon.	راح تحبون يسافرون.
raaH tektiboon kitaab.	راح تكْتِبون كِتاب.
raaH taakhudhoon dewa'.	راح تاخذون دَواء.
leysh taakuloon mnil shaariA?	ليش راح تاكلون منلِشارع؟
leysh raaH titAellimoon Aerebee?	لَيْش راح تِتْعَلِّمون عَرَبي؟
raaH tejlisoon filmeqhaw ktheer.	راح تجلسون في أَلْمَقْهى كثير.
'intoo raaH tesaaAidoon 'ilnaas.	إِنْتو راح تساعْدون إِلْناس.
raaH titfeseHoon kemaan.	راح تِتْفَسَحون كمان.
raaH teSeeroon 'eSdiqaa'.	راح تصيرون أَصْدِقاء.
mish raaH tiHtaajoon shee.	مِش راح تِحْتاجون شي.

❸ Learning Step Three: Speak aloud with new and old sentence patterns.
❹ Learning Step Four: Write as many sentences as you can remember.

➤ Past Tense Verbs: was/used to: kaan كان

Was/were/used to:	kaan	كان
He used to go:	kaan yerooH	هُوَ كان يروح
I used to go:	kuntu 'e·rooH'	أنا كُنتُ أروح
She used to go:	kaanet terooH	هِيَ كانَت تروح
You used to go:	kunt terooH	إِنْتَ كُنت تروح
You (f) used to go:	kunti teroo'·Hi	إِنْتِ كُنتِ تروح
We used to go:	kunaa nerooH	نَحْنُ كُنا نروح
They used to go:	kaanoo yeroo'·Hoon	هُم كانوا يروحون
You (plural) used to go:	kuntum teroo'·Hoon	إِنْتو كُنْتُم تروحون

Summary of the Learned Words in Part Two (192 Words)

Lesson 1:

sleep:	naam	نام
get up:	qoom	قوم
drink:	'ish'·reb	إشرَب
read:	'iq'·re*aa*'	إقرَأ
write:	'ik'·tub	إكْتُب
speak:	'it'·kel·lem	إتْكَلِّم
study:	'ud'·rus	أدْرُس
work:	'ish'·te·ghil	إشْتَغِل
clean:	neZ'·Zif	نَظِّف
love:	Hib	حب
play:	'il'·Aeb	إلْعَب
enjoy:	'it'·me·teA	أتْمَتَع
dream:	'iH'·lem	إحْلَم
brush:	'if'·rish	إفرِش
give:	'iA·Tee'	إعْطي
eat:	kul	كُل
take:	khudh	خُذ
take a shower:	knudh doosh	خُذ دوش
cut:	'iq'·TeA/qe'·tiA	إقْطَع/ قَطِع
freeze something:	fer'·zin	فَرْزِن
thaw something:	dhew'·wib	ذَوِّب
come:	jee' / te'·Aaal	جي/ تَعَال
see:	shoof	شوف
buy:	'ish'·tiree	إشْتِري
want:	reed	ريد
make:	sew'·wee	سَوّي

Lesson 2:

I:	'e·naa'	أنا
see:	shoof	شوف.
I see:	'enaa 'e·shoof'.	أنا أشوف.
I see:	'eshoof.	أشوف.
I want:	'enaa 'e·reed'.	أنا أريد.
I want to see:	'enaa 'ereed 'eshoof.	أنا أريد أشوف.
I want to see:	'ereed 'eshoof.	أريد أشوف.
I sleep:	'enaa 'e·naam'.	أنا أنام.
I sleep:	'enaam.	أنام.
I get up:	'enaa 'e·qoom'.	أنا أقوم.
I drink:	'enaa 'esh'·reb.	أنا أشرَب.
I read:	'enaa 'eq'·re*aa*'.	أنا أقرَأ.

I write:	'enaa 'ek'·tub.	أنا أَكْتُب.
I speak:	'enaa 'et'·kel·lim.	أنا أَتْكَلَّم.
I study:	'enaa 'ed'·rus.	أنا أَدْرُس.
I work:	'enaa 'esh'·tig·hil.	أنا أَشْتِغِل.
I clean:	'enaa 'e'·neZ·Zif.	أنا أَنَظِف.
I love:	'enaa 'e'·Hib.	أنا أَحِب.
I enjoy:	'enaa 'et' me·teA.	أنا أَتْمَتَع.
I dream:	'enaa 'eH'·lem.	أنا أَحْلَم.
I give:	'enaa 'eA·Tee'.	أنا أَعْطي.
I eat:	'enaa 'aa'·kul.	أنا آكُل.
I take:	'enaa 'aa' khudh.	أنا آخُذ.
'enaa	'aakhudh doosh.	أنا آخُذ دوش.
I cut:	'enaa 'e'·qe·TiA.	أنا أَقْطِع.
I freeze:	'enaa 'e'·fer·zin.	أنا أَفَرْزِن.
I thaw:	'enaa 'e'·dhew·wib.	أنا أَذَوِّب.
I come:	'enaa 'e·jee'.	أنا أَجي.
I mean:	'enaa 'eA·nee'.	أنا أَعْني.
I buy:	'enaa 'esh·ti·ree'.	أنا أَشْتِري.
I want to buy:	'e·reed 'eshtiree.	أريد أَشْتِري.
I want to make:	'ereed 'e sew·wee'.	أريد أَسَوّي.
name:	'ism	إسم
my name:	'is·mee'	إسْمي
my name is Jack:	'ismee jaak.	إسْمي جاك.
I am Jack (I jack):	'e·naa' jaak.	أنا جاك.
I am Sue (I Sue):	'e·naa' soo.	أنا سو.
I am happy:	'e·naa' fer·Haan'.	أنا فَرْحان.
the one that:	'il·lee'	إلّي
must/necessary:	laa'·zim	لازم
inside/ in:	prefix bi-	بِ
bigger than the:	'ek'·ber mnil	أَكْبَر مِنِل
that/that is:	he·dhaak'	هَذاك

Lesson 3:

he:	hu'·we	هُوَ
one/someone (m.):	waa'·Hid	واحِد
guy:	shekhS	شَخْص/رَجُل
human being:	'in·saan'	إنْسان
Adam:	aa'·dem	آدَم
Sam:	saam	سام
Jamal:	je·maal'	جَمال
Jack:	jaak	جاك
George:	joorj	جورج

Spoken Arabic for English Speakers

Arabian (m.):	Ae·re·bee′	عَرَبي
Russian (m.):	roo′·see	روسي
American:	′em·ree·kee′	أَمْريكي
teacher (m.):	mu′·Ael·lim	مُعَلِّم
actor:	mu′·me·thil	مُمَثِّل
doctor:	dik·tōor′	دِكْتور
employee:	mu′·we·Zef	مُوَظَّف
chef (m.):	Te·baakh′	طَبَّاخ
dog (m.):	kelb	كَلْب
was (m.):	kaan	كان

Lesson 4:

we:	neH′·nu	نَحْنُ
we sleep:	neH′·nu ne·naam′	نَحْنُ نَنام
we see:	neH′·nu neshoof′	نَحْنُ نشوف
we sleep:	ne·naam′	نَنام
we bring:	neH′·nu nejeeb	نَحْنُ نجيب
people:	naas	ناس
still:	li′ seh	لِسه
not yet:	liseh laa	لِسه لا
not a problem:	mish mush′ ki leh	مِش مُشْكِلَة
certainly:	′e·keed	أكيد
congratulations:	meb·rook′	مَبْروك
very:	ji′·den	جِداً
office:	′ōo′ fees	أوْفيس
helicopter:	hi li kōob′ ter	هِلِكوبْتَر
the pyramids:	′el ′eh raam′	ألأهْرام

Lesson 5:

she:	hi′·ye	هِيَ
Nadia:	naa′·di·yaa	ناديا
je·mee′·leh		جَميلَة
ley′·law		لَيْلى
language:	lu′·gheh (f.)	لُغَة
human being (m.):	in·saan′	إنْسان
human being (f.):	in·saa′·neh	إنْسانة
a country (f.):	de′·wleh	دَوْلَة
important (m.):	mu′·him	مُهِم
important (f.):	mu′·hi·meh	مُهِمَة
balcony:	baal′·kōon	بالْكون
a dress:	fus·taan′	فُسْتان
she wears:	hiya til′·bes	هِيَ تِلْبَس

she sleeps:	hiya tenaam'	هِيَ تنام
she sees:	hiya teshoof'	هِيَ تشوف
she brings:	hiya tejeeb	هِيَ تجيب

Lesson 6:
you (m.):	'in'·te	إنْتَ
you want:	'inte tereed	إنْتَ تريد
Do you want?:	'inte tereed?	إنْتَ تريد؟
I have:	Ain·dee'	عِنْدي
mall:	sooq/mōol	سوق/ مول
medication:	de·waa''	دَواء
Aspirin:	'es·pi·reen'	أسْبِرين
toilet papers:	we'·req ti·waa'·leyt	وَرَق تِواليت
penicillin:	ben·se·leen'	بَنْسَلين
pain:	'e'·lem	ألَم
diabetes:	suk'·ker	سُكَّر
AIDS test:	feHA 'eydz	فَحْص أيْدْز

Lesson 7:
you (feminine):	'in'·ti	إنْتِ
you want:	'inti tereed'·i	إنْتِ تريدِ
Do you want?:	'inte tereedi?	إنْتِ تريدِ؟
you bring:	'inti tejee'·bi	إنْتِ تجيبِ
you sleep:	'inti tenaa'·mi	إنْتِ تنامِ
you see:	'inti teshoo'·fi	إنْتِ تشوفِ
you buy:	'inti tish'·ti·ri	إنْتِ تِشتِر
you walk:	'inti tim'·shi	إنْتِ تِمْشِ
be (feminine):	koo'·nee	كوني
you (f.) become:	'inti tekoo'·ni	إنْتِ تكونِ
friend:	Se·deeq'	صَديق
friends:	'eS·di·qaa'	أصْدِقاء
friend (f.):	Se·dee'·qeh	صَديقَة
verb:	fiAl	فِعْل
do:	'if'·Ael	إفْعَل
do (f.):	'if'·Ae·li	إفْعَلِ

Lesson 8:
they:	hum	هُم
they want:	hum yeree'·doon	هُم يريدون
they don't want:	hum laa yereedoon	هُم لا يريدون
they speak:	hum yi·tekel·li·moon'	هُم بِتْكَلِّمون
go down/get off:	'in'·zil	إنْزِل

they get off:	hum yenziloon	هُم ينزلون
friends:	'eS·di·qaa'	أصْدِقاء
relatives:	'e·qaa'·rib	أقارب
'eSdiqaa we'eqaarib yijoon		أصْدِقاء وأقارب يِجون

Lesson 9:

you (plural):	'in·too'	إنْتو
you (p.) sleep:	'intoo tenaa'·moon	إنْتو تنامون
you (p.) bring:	'intoo tejee'·boon	إنْتو تجيبون
you (p.) want:	'intoo teree'·doon	إنْتو تريدون
you (p.) speak:	'intoo ti·tekel·li·moon'	إنْتو تِتْكلّمون
you (p.) get off:	'intoo tenzi·loon'	إنْتو تنزلون
you (p.) say:	'intoo teqoo'·loon	إنْتو تقولون
you (p.) be:	'intoo tekoo'·noon	إنْتو تكونون
you (p.) become:	'intoo teSee'·roon	إنْتو تصيرون
you (p.) are friends:	'intoo 'eS·di·qaa'	إنْتو أصْدِقاء
you (p.) are relatives:	'intoo 'e·qaa'·rib	إنْتو أقارب
a thing:	shee	شي

Lesson 10:

will: raaH راح

I will go: raaH 'e·rooH أنا راح أروح   He will go: raaH yerooH هُوَ راح يروح
She will go: raaH terooH هِيَ راح تروح   You will go: raaH terooH إنْتَ راح تروح
You (f) will go: raaH teroo·Hi إنْتِ راح تروحي   We will go: raaH nerooH نَحْنُ راح نروح
They will go: raaH yeroo·Hoon هُم راح يروحون   You (plural) will go: 'entum raaH teroo·Hoon أنْتُو راح تروحون

➤Arabic text is written without short vowels, except in very formal or religious settings. Outside of this book, this is how Arabic text will look like. Familiarize yourself by seeing Arabic text without the short vowels. Place the short vowels (حَرَكات) and other Arabic symbols on this Arabic text you have learned:

'enaa raaH 'ejeeb ruzz.	أنا راح أجيب رز.
'enaa raaH 'esewwee shaay.	أنا راح أسوي شاي.
'enaa raaH 'eshreb shaay.	أنا راح أشرب شاي.
'enaa raaH 'erooH lilsooq.	أنا راح أروح للسوق.
raaH 'ejee lilbeyt.	راح أجي للبيت.
daa'imen raaH 'esaafir.	دائما راح أسافر.
daa'imen raaH 'ezoor 'elmetHef.	دائما راح أزور المتحف.
raaH 'eshoof mekaan kebeer.	راح أشوف مكان كبير.
raaH 'ejeeb shaay wekeyk.	راح أجيب شاي وكيك.
raaH 'ejeeb shaay wekeyk.	أجيب شاي وأجيب كيك.
'enaa 'illee raaH 'ejeeb elkeyk.	أنا إللي راح أجيب ألكيك.
daa'men raaH 'ejeeb keyk.	دائما أجيب كيك.

'enaa 'illee raaH 'esewwee 'ilshaay.	أنا إللي راح أسوي ألشاي.
huwe raaH raaH yejeeb ruzz.	هو راح يجيب رز.
huwe raaH yesewwee shaay.	هو راح يسوي شاي.
huwe raaH yeshreb shaay.	هو راح يشرب شاي.
huwe raaH yerooH lilsooq.	هو راح يروح للسوق.
raaH yejee lilbeyt.	راح يجي للبيت.
huwe raaH yesaafir daa'imen.	هو راح يسافر دائما.
huwe raaH yezoor 'elmetHef.	هو راح يزور المتحف.
raaH yetkellem Aerebee.	راح يتكلم عربي.
raaH yeshoof mekaan kebeer.	راح يشوف مكان كبير.
huwe raaH yejeeb keyk.	هو راح يجيب كيك.
raaH yejeeb shaay wekeyk.	راح يجيب شاي وكيك.
raaH yesewwee 'ilshaay.	راح يسوي الشاي.
raaH yetkellem Aerebee.	راح يتكلم عربي.
aadem raaH yedrus fee miSr.	آدم راح يدرس في مصر.
saam raaH yishteghil muweZef.	سام راح يشتغل موظف.
jaak raaH yeTbukh 'ekl ledheedh	جاك راح يطبخ أكل لذيذ.
joorj raaH yaakul 'ekl Aerebee	جورج راح يأكل أكل عربي.
'ilmuAellim raaH yeSeer mumethil.	المعلم راح يصير ممثل.
neHnu raaH nejeeb ruzz.	نحن راح نجيب رز.
neHnu raaH nesewwee shaay.	نحن راح نسوي شاي.
raaH nishreb shaay.	راح نشرب شاي.
raaH nedrus Hisaab.	راح ندرس حساب.
neHnu raaH nitkellem ketheer.	نحن راح نتكلم كثير.
neHnu raaH nerooH lilsooq.	نحن راح نروح للسوق.
raaH nejee lilbeyt.	راح نجي للبيت.
neHnu raaH daa'imen nesaafir.	نحن راح دائما نسافر.
daa'imen raaH nezoor 'elmetHef.	دائما راح نزور المتحف.
raaH nitkellem Aerebee.	راح نتكلم عربي.
raaH neshoof mekaan kebeer.	راح نشوف مكان كبير.
neHnu 'illee raaH nejeeb'elkeyk.	نحن إللي راح نجيب ألكيك.
raaH nesewwee 'ilshaay.	راح نسوي الشاي.
raaH nitkellem Aerebee.	راح نتكلم عربي.
'enaa weaadem raaH nedrus.	أنا وآدم راح ندرس.
raaH neshoof 'ilHraam.	راح نشوف الأهرام.
'enaa wejemaal nejeeb mey.	مش مشكلة، أنا وجمال راح نجيب مي.
raaH nishteghil.	راح نشتغل.
raaH naakul beyD.	راح نأكل بيض.
raaH nitkillim Aerebee	راح نتكلم عربي.
neHnu raaH neTbukh.	نحن راح نطبخ.

hiye raaH tejeeb ruzz.	هي راح تجيب رز.
hiye raaH tesewwee shaay.	هي راح تسوي شاي.
hiye raaH tishreb shaay.	هي راح تشرب شاي.
hiye raaH tedrus Hisaab.	هي راح تدرس حساب.
hiye raaH titkellem ketheer.	هي راح تتكلم كثير.
hiye raaH terooH lilsooq.	هي راح تروح للسوق.
hiye raaH tejee lilbeyt daa'imen.	هي راح تجي للبيت دائماً.
hiye raaH daa'imen tesaafir.	هي راح دائماً تسافر.
daa'imen hiye raaH tezoor 'elmetHef.	دائماً هي راح تزور المتحف.
hiye raaH titkellem Aerebee.	هي راح تتكلم عربي.
raaH teshoof mekaan kebeer.	لازم تشوف مكان كبير.
hiye raaH tejeeb keyk.	هي راح تجيب كيك.
hiye 'illee raaH tesewwee 'ilshaay.	هي إللي راح تسوي الشاي.
naadiyaa raaH tidrus fee 'ilbaalkōon.	نادياً تدرس في البالكون.
jemeeleh raaH tilbes fustaan jemeel.	جميلة راح تلبس فستان جميل.
hiye raaH tesaafir lidewleh Aerebiyeh.	هي راح تسافر لدولة عربية.
raaH tiktib kitaab lugheh Aerebiyeh.	هي راح تكتب كتاب لغة عربية.
'inte raaH tejeeb ruzz.	إنت راح تجيب رز.
'inte raaH tesewwee shaay.	إنت راح تسوي شاي.
'inte raaH tishreb shaay.	إنت راح تشرب شاي.
'inte raaH laa tedrus Hisaab.	إنت راح لا تدرس حساب.
'inte raaH titkellem ketheer.	إنت راح تتكلم كثير.
'inte raaH terooH lilsooq.	إنت راح تروح للسوق.
'inte raaH tejee lilbeyt daa'imen.	إنت راح تجي للبيت دائماً.
'inte raaH daa'imen tesaafir.	إنت راح دائماً تسافر.
raaH terooH lilmetHef.	راح تروح للمتحف.
raaH titkellem Aerebee.	راح تتكلم عربي.
teshoof mekaan kebeer.	راح تشوف مكان كبير.
'inte 'illee raaH tejeeb 'elkeyk.	إنت إللي راح تجيب ألكيك.
'inte 'illee raaH tesewwee 'ilshaay.	إنت إللي راح تسوي ألشاي.
raaH tidrus fee 'ilbaalkōon?	راح تدرس في البالكون؟
raaH tijee Aindee?	راح تجي عندي؟
raaH tiktib kitaab.	راح تكتب كتاب.
meen raaH tiktib?	مين راح تكتب كتاب؟
'inte raaH tiktib 'ew hiye raaH tiktib?	إنت راح تكتب أو هي راح تكتب؟
'inte raaH taakhudh dewa'?	إنت راح تاخذ دواء؟
raaH aakhudh dewaa' sukker.	راح آخذ دواء سكر.
raaH taakul 'ekl mnil shaariA?	راح تاكل أكل منلشارع؟
lesh raaH titAellim Aerebee?	ليش راح تتعلم عربي؟
'inte raaH tesaaAid 'ilnaas ktheer.	إنت راح تساعد إلناس كثير.

raaH tekoon kemaa 'inte.	راح تكون كما أنت.
'inti raaH raaH tejeebi ruzz.	إنت راح تجيب رز.
'inti raaH tesewwee shaay.	إنت راح تسوي شاي.
'inti raaH tishrebi shaay.	إنت راح تشرب شاي.
'inti raaH laa tedrusi Hisaab.	إنت راح لا تدرس حساب.
'inti raaH titkellemi ketheer.	إنت راح تتكلم كثير.
'inti raaH terooHi lilsooq.	إنت راح تروح للسوق.
'inti raaH tejee lilbeyt daa'imen.	إنت راح تجي للبيت دائما.
'inti raaH daa'imen tesaafiri.	إنت راح دائما تسافر.
'inti raaH titkellemi Aerebee.	إنت راح تتكلم عربي.
raaH teshoofi mekaan kebeer.	راح تشوف مكان كبير.
'inti raaH tejeebi keyk.	إنت راح تجيب كيك.
mish 'inti 'illee raaH tejeebi 'elkeyk.	مش إنت إللي راح تجيب ألكيك.
'inti 'illee raaH tesewwee 'ilshaay.	إنت إللي راح تسوي ألشاي.
raaH tidrusi fee 'ilbaalkoon?	راح تدرس في ألبالكون؟
raaH tiktibi kitaab?	راح تكتب كتاب؟
raaH tejee Aindee?	راح تجي عندي؟
raaH taakhudhi 'esbireen?	راح تاخذ أسبرين؟
raaH taakuli 'ekl mnil shaariA?	راح تاكل أكل منلشارع؟
raaH tijlisi filmeqhaw ktheer?	راح تجلس في ألمقهى كثير؟
raaH teHibi meqhaw 'ilfeeshaawee?	راح تحب مقهى إلفيشاوي؟
'inti raaH tesaaAidi 'ilnaas ktheer.	إنت راح تساعد إلناس كثير.
hum raaH yejeeboon ruzz.	هم راح يجيبون رز.
hum raaH yesewwoon shaay.	هم راح يسوون شاي.
hum raaH yishreboon shaay.	هم راح يشربون شاي.
hum raaH yitkellemoom ketheer.	هم راح يتكلمون كثير.
hum raaH yerooHoon lilsooq.	هم راح يروحون للسوق.
hum raaH yejoon lilbeyt daa'imen.	هم راح يجون للبيت دائما.
hum raaH daa'imen yesaafiroon.	هم راح دائما يسافرون.
hum raaH yitkellemoon Aerebee.	هم راح يتكلمون عربي.
raaH yeshoofoon mekaan kebeer.	راح يشوفون مكان كبير.
hum raaH yejeeboon keyk.	هم راح يجيبون كيك.
hum 'illee raaH yejeeboon 'elkeyk.	هم إللي راح يجيبون ألكيك.
hum raaH yesewwoon 'ilshaay.	هم راح يسوون ألشاي.
'ekeed raaH yesewwoon 'ilshaay.	أكيد راح يسوون ألشاي.
raaH yedrusoon fee 'ilbaalkōon.	راح يدرسون في ألبالكون.
raaH yeHiboon yesaafiroon.	راح يحبون يسافرون.
raaH yektiboon kitaab.	راح يكتبون كتاب.
raaH yaakhudhoon dewa'.	راح ياخذون دواء.
leysh yaakuloon mnil shaariA?	ليش راح ياكلون منلشارع؟

leysh raaH yitAellimoon Aerebee?   ليش راح يتعلمون عربي؟
raaH yijlisoon filmeqhaw ktheer.   راح يجلسون في ألمقهى كثير.
raaH yeHiboon meqhaw 'ilfeeshaawee.   راح يحبون مقهى إلفيشاوي.
hum raaH yesaaAidoon 'ilnaas.   هم راح يساعدون إلناس.
raaH yitfeseHoon kemaan.   راح يتفسحون كمان.
raaH yeSeeroon 'eSdiqaa',   راح يصيرون أصدقاء.
mish raaH yiHtaajoon shee.   مش راح يحتاجون شي.

'intoo raaH tejeeboon ruzz.   إنتو راح تجيبون رز.
'intoo raaH tesewwoon shaay.   إنتو راح تسوون شاي.
'intoo raaH tishreboon shaay.   إنتو راح تشربون شاي.
'intoo raaH titkellemoom ketheer.   إنتو راح تتكلمون كثير.
'intoo raaH terooHoon lilsooq.   إنتو راح تروحون للسوق.
'intoo raaH tejoon lilbeyt daa'imen.   إنتو راح تجون للبيت دائما.
'intoo raaH daa'imen tesaafiroon.   إنتو راح دائما تسافرون.
'intoo raaH titkellemoon Aerebee.   إنتو راح تتكلمون عربي.
raaH teshoofoon mekaan kebeer.   راح تشوفون مكان كبير.
'intoo raaH tejeeboon keyk.   إنتو راح تجيبون كيك.
'intoo 'illee raaH tejeeboon 'elkeyk.   إنتو إللي راح تجيبون ألكيك.
'intoo raaH tesewwoon 'ilshaay.   إنتو راح تسوون ألشاي.
'ekeed raaH tesewwoon 'ilshaay.   أكيد راح تسوون ألشاي.
raaH tedrusoon fee 'ilbaalkōon.   راح تدرسون في ألبالكون.
raaH teHiboon tesaafiroon.   راح تحبون يسافرون.
raaH tektiboon kitaab.   راح تكتبون كتاب.
raaH taakhudhoon dewa'.   راح تاخذون دواء.
leysh taakuloon mnil shaariA?   ليش راح تاكلون منلشارع؟
leysh raaH titAellimoon Aerebee?   ليش راح تتعلمون عربي؟
raaH tejlisoon filmeqhaw ktheer.   راح تجلسون في ألمقهى كثير.
raaH teHiboon meqhaw 'ilfeeshaawee.   راح تحبون مقهى إلفيشاوي.
'intoo raaH tesaaAidoon 'ilnaas.   إنتو راح تساعدون إلناس.
raaH titfeseHoon kemaan.   راح تتفسحون كمان.
raaH teSeeroon 'eSdiqaa',   راح تصيرون أصدقاء.
mish raaH tiHtaajoon shee.   مش راح تحتاجون شي.

Assuming you are also studying the alphabet book by Camilia Sadik entitled *The Arabic Alphabet for English Speakers by Camilia Sadik*, write these words using Arabic letters, as in naam: نام

sleep: naam _____نام_____   I sleep: 'enaam _____
He sleeps: yenaam _____   We sleep: nenaam _____
She sleeps: tenaam _____   You sleep: tenaam _____
You (f.) sleep: tenaami _____   They sleep: yenaamoon _____
You (p.) sleep: tenaamoon _____   I will sleep: raaH 'enaam _____

see: shoof _____
He sees: yeshoof _____
She sees: teshoof _____
You (f.) see: teshoofi _____
You (p.) see: teshoofoon _____

I see: 'eshoof _____
We see: neshoof _____
You see: teshoof _____
They see: yeshoofoon _____
He will see: raaH yeshoof

bring: jeeb _____
He brings: yejeeb _____
She brings: tejeeb _____
You (f.) bring: tejeebi _____
You (p.) bring: tejeeboon _____

I bring: 'ejeeb _____
We bring: nejeeb _____
You bring: tejeeb _____
They bring: yejeeboon _____
We will bring: raaH nejeeb

want: reed _____
He wants: yereed _____
She wants: tereed _____
You (f.) want: tereedi _____
You (p.) want: tereedoon _____

I want: 'ereed _____
We want: nereed _____
You want: tereed _____
They want: yereedoon _____
She'll want: raaH tereed _____

come: jee/teAaal _____
He comes: yejee _____
She comes: tejee _____
You (f.) come: tejee _____
You (p.) come: tejeeoon _____

I come: 'ejee _____
We come: nejee _____
You come: tejee _____
They come: yejeeoon _____
You'll come: raaH tejee _____

walk: 'imshee _____
He walks: yemshee _____
She walks: temshee _____
You (f.) walk: temshee _____
You (p.) walk: temshoon _____

I walk: 'emshee _____
We walk: nemshee _____
You walk: temshee _____
They walk: yemshoon _____
You (f) will walk: raaH temshee _____

give: 'iATee _____
He gives: yeATee _____
She gives: teATee _____
You (f.) give: teATee _____
You (p.) give: teAToon _____

I give: 'eATee _____
We give: neATee _____
You give: teATee _____
They give: yeAToon _____
They'll give: raaH yeAToon _____

take: khudh _____
He takes: yaakhudh _____
She takes: taakhudh _____
You (f.) take: taakhudhi _____
You (p.) take: taakhdhoon _____
eat: kul _____

I take: aakhudh _____
We take: naakhudh _____
You take: taakudh _____
They take: yaakhdhoon _____
You (p.) will take: raaH taakhdhoon _____
I eat: aakul _____

Spoken Arabic for English Speakers

He eats: yaakul _____
She eats: taakul _____
You (f.) eat: taakhuli _____
You (p.) eat: taakloon _____

I need: 'eHtaaj _____
We play: nelAeb _____
You use: testeAmil _____
They write: yektiboon _____

I talk: 'eHkee _____
We enjoy: netmeteA _____
You talk: tiHkee _____
They cook: yeTbikhoon _____

I have: Aindee _____
We enjoy: netmeteA _____
You visit: tezoor _____
They drink: yeshreboon _____

I love: 'eHib _____
We dream: neHlem _____
You brush: tifrish _____
They love: yeHiboon _____

We eat: naakul _____
You eat: taakul _____
They eat: yaakloon _____
talk: 'iHkee _____

He means: yeAnee _____
She hears: tismeA _____
You (f.) speak: titkellimi _____
You (p.) need: teHtaajoon _____

He goes out for fun: yitfeseH _____
She asks for: tiTlub _____
You (f.) travel: tezoori _____
You (p.) sit: tejlisoon _____

He becomes: yeSeer _____
She asks for: tiTlub _____
You (f.) be: tekooni _____
You (p.) buy: tishtiroon _____

He gets up: yeqoom _____
She cuts: tiqeTiA _____
You (f.) thaw: tedhewibi _____
You (p.) freeze: tiferzinoon _____

Make your own Sentences!

Say each of these words in a sentence or a phrase:

naam نام
'iqreaa' إقرَأ
'udrus أُدْرُس
Hib حِب
'iH·lem إحْلَم
kul كُل
ferzin فَرْزن
shoof شوف
sewwee سَوّي

qoom قوم
'iktub إكْتُب
'ishteghil إشْتَغِل
'ilAeb إلْعَب
'ifrish إفْرِش
khudh خُذ
dhewwib ذَوِّب
'ishtiree إشْتِري
knudh doosh خُذ دوش

'ishreb إشرَب
'itkellem إتْكَلِّم
neZ·Zif نَظَّف
'itmeteA إتْمَتَع
'iATee إعْطي
'iqTeA إقْطَع
jee' / teAaal جي/ تَعَال
reed ريد

'enaa أنا
'enaam أَنام
'eqreaa' أَقرأ

'eshoof أشوف
'eqoom أقوم
'ektub أَكْتُب

'ereed أريد
'eshreb أشرَب
'etkellim أتْكَلِّم

Spoken Arabic for English Speakers

'edrus أَدْرُس	'eshtighil أَشْتِغِل	'eneZZif أَنَظِّف
'eHib أَحِب	'etmeteA أَتْمَتَع	'eHlem أَحْلَم
'eATee أَعْطي	'aakul آكُل	'aakhudh آخُذ
aakhudh doosh آخُذ دوش	'eqeTiA أَقَطِع	'eferzin أَفْرزن
'edhewwib أَذَوِّب	'ejee أَجي	'eAnee أَعْني
'eshtiree أَشْتَري	'ism إِسْم	'ismee إِسْمي
'ismee إِسْمي	'enaa soo أنا سو	hedhaak هَذاك
'ereed 'eshtiree أريد أَشْتَري	'ereed 'eshoof أريد أشوف	

huwe هُوَ	waaHid واحِد	shekhS/rejul شَخْص/رَجُل
'insaan إنْسان	kaan كان	yenaam ينام
yeqoom يقوم	yeshreb يشرَب	yeqreaa' يقرأ
yektub يكْتُب	yetkellim يتْكَلِّم	yedrus يدْرُس
yeshtighil يشْتِغِل	yeneZZif ينَظِّف	yeHib يحِب
yetmeteA يتْمَتَع	yiHlem يِحْلَم	yeATee يعْطي
yaakul ياكُل	yaakhudh ياخُذ	yeqeTiA يقَطِع
yeferzin يفَرْزن	yejee يجي	yeAnee يعْني
yishtiree يشْتَري	yereed yeshtiree يريد يشْتَري	yereed yeshoof يريد يشوف

neHnu نَحْنُ	nenaam نَحْنُ نَنام	neshoof نشوف
nejeeb نجيب	naas ناس	liseh لِسه
liseh laa لِسه لا	mish mushkileh مِش مُشْكِلَة	'ekeed أكيد
mebrook مَبْروك	jiden جِداً	'ōofees أوفيس
hilikōobter هِلِكوبْتَر	'el'ehraam ألأَهْرام	nereed neshoof

hiye هِيَ	naadiyaa ناديا	jemeeleh جَميلَة
leylaw لَيلى	lugheh لُغَة	insaan إنْسان
insaaneh إنْسانَة	dewleh دَوْلَة	muhim مُهِم
muhimeh مُهِمَة	baalkōon بالْكون	fustaan فُسْتان
hiya tilbes هِيَ تِلْبَس	hiya teshoof هِيَ تشوف	hiya tejeeb هِيَ تجيب

'inte إنْتَ	'inte tereed إنْتَ تريد	Aindee
sooq/mōol سوق/مول	dewaa' دَواء	'espireen أَسْبِرين
wereq tiwaaleyt وَرَق تواليت	benseleen بَنْسَلين	'elem أَلَم

'inti إنْتِ	'inti tereedi إنْتِ تريدِ	'inti tejeebi إنْتِ تجيبِ
'inti tenaami إنْتِ تنامِ	'inti teshoofi إنْتِ تشوفِ	'inti tishtiri إنْتِ تِشْتِرِ
'inti timshi إنْتِ تِمْشِ	koonee كوني	'inti tekooni إنْتِ تكونِ
Sedeeq صَديق	'eSdiqaa أَصْدِقاء	Sedeeqeh صَديقَة
fiAl فِعْل	'ifAel إفْعَل	'ifAeli إفْعَلِ

hum هُم	hum yereedoon هُم يريدون	yitekellimoon يتْكَلِّمون

'eqaarib أقارب   eSdiqaa' أَصْدِقاء   hum yenziloon هُم ينزلون

'intoo إنْتو
'intoo tejeeboon إنْتو تجيبون
'intoo titekellimoon إنْتو تِتْكَلّمون
'intoo teqooloon إنْتو تقولون
'intoo teSeeroon إنْتو تصيرون
'intoo 'eqaarib إنْتو أقارب

'intoo tenaamoon إنْتو تنامون
'intoo tereedoon إنْتو تريدون
'intoo tenziloon إنْتو تنزلون
'intoo tekoonoon إنْتو تكونون
'intoo 'eSdiqaa' إنْتو أَصْدِقاء
shee شي

raaH راح
huwe raaH yerooH هُوَ راح يروح
'inte raaH terooH إنْتَ راح تروح
neHnu raaH nerooH نَحْنُ راح نروح
'entum raaH terooHoon أَنْتُم راح تروحون

'enaa raaH 'e·rooH أنا راح أروح
hiye raaH terooH هِيَ راح تروح
'inti raaH terooHi إنْتِ راح تروحِ
hum raaH yerooHoon هُم راح يروحون

Spoken Arabic for English Speakers

Practice Quiz

Translate the following into Arabic:

sleep	get up	drink	read
write	speak	study	work
clean	love	play	enjoy
dream	brush	give	eat
take	cut	freeze	thaw
come	see	buy	want
make	I sleep	he sees	we want
she visits	you walk	you (f.) visit	they say goodbye
you (p.) sit	I will speak	he will talk	she wants

I see	I want	I want to see	I sleep
I get up	I drink	I read	I write
I speak	I talk	I study	I work
I clean	I love	I enjoy	I dream
I give	I eat	I take	I take a shower
I cut	I freeze	I come	I mean
I buy	I want to buy	I want to make	name
my name is	the one that	I'm happy	must
bigger than the	that/that is	I have	that

---

he	one	guy	human being
Adam	George	Arabian (m.)	Russian (m.)
American	teacher (m.)	actor	doctor
employee	chef (m.)	dog (m.)	was
he gets up	he drinks	he reads	he writes
he speaks	he plays	he studies	he works
he cleans	he loves	he enjoys	he dreams
he gives	he eats	he takes	he takes a shower
he cuts	he freezes	he comes	he means
he buys	he wants to buy	he wants to make	

---

we	we sleep	we see	we bring
people	still	not yet	not a problem
certainly	very	office	congratulations
helicopter	the pyramids	we bring	we eat
we get up	we drink	we read	we write
we speak	we play	we study	we work
we clean	we love	we enjoy	we dream
we give	we eat	we take	we take a shower
we cut	we freeze	we come	we mean

we buy	we want to buy	we want to make	
she	Nadia	jemeeleh	leylaw
language	a country	human being (m.)	human being (f.)
important (m.)	important (f.)	balcony	she sleeps
she wears	a dress	she sees	she brings
she gets up	she drinks	she reads	she writes
she speaks	she plays	she studies	she works
she cleans	she loves	she enjoys	she dreams
she gives	she eats	she takes	she takes a shower
she cuts	she freezes	she comes	she means
she buys	she wants to buy	she wants to make	
you (m.)	you want	you sleep	you bring
you buy	you walk	mall	medication
Aspirin	pain	diabetes	toilet paper
you get up	you drink	you read	you write
you speak	you play	you study	you work
you clean	you love	you enjoy	you dream
you give	you eat	you take	you take a shower
you cut	you freeze	you come	you mean
you buy	you want to buy	you want to make	
you (f.)	you want	you sleep	you bring
you buy	you walk	you be	you become
a friend (m.)	a friend (f.)	friends	verb
do	do (f.)	he does	she does
you get up	you drink	you read	you write
you speak	you play	you study	you work
you clean	you love	you enjoy	you dream
you give	you eat	you take	you take a shower
you cut	you freeze	you come	you mean
you buy	you want to buy	you want to make	
they	they want	they sleep	they see
they don't want	go down/get off	they go down	they speak
they get up	they drink	they read	they write
they play	they talk	they study	they work
they clean	they love	they enjoy	they dream
they give	they eat	they take	they take a shower
they cut	they freeze	they come	they mean
they buy	they want to buy	they want to make	

you (plural)	you (p.) sleep	you (p.) bring	you (p.) want
you (p.) speak	you (p.) get off	you (p.) say	you (p.) sleep
you (p.) see	you (p.) love	you (p.) eat	you (p.) take
you (p.) buy	you (p.) come	you (p.) become	you (p.) want to buy

will	I will go	he'll go	she'll go
you'll go	you (f) will go	we'll go	they'll go
you (plural) will go	I will sleep	he'll sleep	she'll sleep
you'll sleep	you (f) will sleep	we'll sleep	they'll sleep
you (plural) will sleep	I will eat	he'll eat	she'll eat
you'll eat	you (f) will eat	we'll eat	they'll eat
you (plural) will eat	he'll take	she'll play	we'll bring

Spoken Arabic for English Speakers

Chart of Verb Conjugations

I: 'enaa أنا	He: huwe هُوَ	We: neHnu نَحْنُ	She: hiye هَيَ	You: 'inte إنْتَ	You: 'inti إنْتِ	They: hum هُم
'enaam	yenaam	nenaam	tenaam	tenaam	tenaami	yenaamoon
'ejeeb	yejeeb	nejeeb	tejeeb	tejeeb	tejeebi	yejeeboon
'eshoof	yeshoof	neshoof	teshoof	teshoof	teshoofi	yeshoofoon
'erooH	yerooH	nerooH	terooH	terooH	terooHi	yerooHoon
'esewwee	yesewwee	nesewwee	tesewwee	tesewwee	tesewwee	yesewwoon
'emshee	yemshee	nemshee	temshee	temshee	temshee	yemshoon
'eqool	yeqool	neqool	teqool	teqool	teqooli	yeqooloon
'eqoom	yeqoom	neqoom	teqoom	teqoom	teqoomi	yeqoomoon
'eHkee	yeHkee	neHkee	teHkee	teHkee	teHkee	yeHkoon
'eHtaaj	yeHtaaj	neHtaaj	teHtaaj	teHtaaj	teHtaaji	yeHtaajoon
'elAeb	yelAeb	nelAeb	telAeb	telAeb	telAebi	yelAeboon
'ereed	yereed	nereed	tereed	tereed	tereedi	yereedoon
'eHis	yeHis	neHis	teHis	teHis	teHisi	yeHisoon
'efekir	yefekir	nefekir	tefekir	tefekir	tefekiri	yefekiroon
'esteAmil	yesteAmil	nesteAmil	testeAmil	testeAmil	testeAmili	yesteAmiloon
'eATee	yeATee	neATee	teATee	teATee	teATee	yeAToon
'eHib	yeHib	neHib	teHib	teHib	teHibi	yeHiboon
'ezoor	yezoor	nezoor	tezoor	tezoor	tezoori	yezooroon
'eneZZif	yenZZif	nenZZif	tenZZif	tenZZif	tenZZifi	yenZZifoon
'ekoon	yekoon	nekoon	tekoon	tekoon	tekooni	yekoonoon
'emlik	yemlik	nemlik	temlik	temlik	temliki	yemlikoon
'esheel	yesheel	nesheel	tesheel	tesheel	tesheeli	yesheeloon
'eSeer	yeSeer	neSeer	teSeer	teSeer	teSeeri	yeSeeroon
'eHuT	yeHuT	neHuT	teHuT	teHuT	teHuTi	yeHuToon
aakul	yaakul	naakul	taakul	taakul	taakuli	yaakuloon
aakhudh	yaakhudh	naakhudh	taakhudh	taakhudh	taakhudhi	yaakhudhoon
'etkellim	yitkellim	nitkellim	titkellim	titkellim	titkellimi	yitkellimoon
'etAllem	yitAllem	nitAllem	titAllem	titAllem	titAllemi	yitAllemoon
'esmeA	yismeA	nismeA	tismeA	tismeA	tismeAi	yismeAoon
'ektib	yiktib	niktib	tiktib	tiktib	tiktibi	yiktiboon
'eTlib	yiTlub	niTlub	tiTlub	tiTlub	tiTlubi	yiTluboon
'edrus	yidrus	nidrus	tidrus	tidrus	tidrusi	yidrusoon
'eTbukh	yiTbukh	niTbukh	tiTbukh	tiTbukh	tiTbukhi	yiTbukhoon
'eqreaa'	yiqreaa'	niqreaa'	tiqreaa'	tiqreaa'	tiqreaa'ee	yiqreaa'oon
'eAnee	yiAnee	niAnee	tiAnee	tiAnee	tiAnee	yiAnoon
'etmeteA	yitmeteA	nitmeteA	titmeteA	titmeteA	titmeteAi	yitmeteAoon
'etfeseH	yitfeseH	nitfeseH	titfeseH	titfeseH	titfeseHi	yitfeseHoon
'elbes	yilbis	nilbis	tilbis	tilbis	tilbisi	yilbisoon
'etferej	yitferej	nitferej	titferej	titferej	titfereji	yitferejoon
'eshrub	yishrub	nishrub	tishrub	tishrub	tishrubi	yishruboon
'eshtughul	yishtughul	nishtughul	tishtughul	tishtughul	tishtughuli	yishtughloon
'enzil	yinzil	ninzil	tinzil	tinzil	tinzili	yinziloon
'eghsil	yighsil	nighsil	tighsil	tighsil	tighsili	yighsiloon
'efAel	yifAel	nifAel	tifAel	tifAel	tifAeli	yefAeloon

Spoken Arabic for English Speakers

Chart of Learned Words in Four Major Arabic Dialects

Learned Words	Egypt	Mediterranean	Gulf	FuSHaw
I أنا	'enaa أنا	'enaa أنا	'aanee آ	'enaa أنا
'ismee إسْمي	'ismee إسْمي	'ismee إسْمي	'ismee إسْمي	'ismee إسْمي
'illee إلّي	'illee إلّي	'illee إلّي	'illee إلّي	'eledhee ألّذي
hinaak هِناك	hinaak هِناك	hnaak هناك	hnaak هناك	hunaak هُناك
'ekber mnil أكْبَر مْنِل	'ekber mnil أكْبَر مْنِل	'ekber mnil أكْبَر مْنِل	'ekber mnil أكْبَر مْنِل	'ekber min 'el
laazim لازم	laazim لازم	laazim لازم	laazim لازم	laazim لازم
huwe هُوَ	huwwe هُوَّ	huwwe هُوَّ	huwwe هُوَّ	huwe هُوَ
waaHid واحِد	waaHid واحِد	waaHed واحَد	waaHid واحِد	waaHid واحِد
'insaan إنْسان	'insaan إنْسان	'insaan إنْسان	'insaan إنْسان	'insaan إنْسان
Aeraabee عَرَبي	Aeraabee عَرَبي	Aeraabee عَرَبي	Aeraabee عَرَبي	Aeraabee عَرَبي
'inkileezee إنْكليزي	ingleezee إنْكليزي	ingleezee إنْكليزي	'inkileezee إنْكليزي	'injileezee إنْجِليزي
muAellim مُعَلِّم	muAellim مُعَلِّم	muAellim مُعَلِّم	muAellim مُعَلِّم	muAellim مُعَلِّم
mumethil مُمَثِّل	mumesil مُمَسِّل	mumetil مُمَتِّل	mumethil مُمَثِّل	mumethil مُمَثِّل
muweZef مُوَظَّف	muwezef مُوَزَّف	muwedef مُوَدَّف	muweZef مُوَظَّف	muweZef مُوَظَّف
Tebaakh طَبَّاخ	Tebaakh طَبَّاخ	Tebaakh طَبَّاخ	Tebaakh طَبَّاخ	Tebaakh طَبَّاخ
kelb كَلْب	kelb كَلْب	kelib كَلِب	kelb كَلْب	kelb كَلْب
kaan كان	kaan كان	kaan كان	chaan جان	kaane كانَ
hum هُم	hum هُم	hume هُمَ	hume هُمَ	hum هُم
naas ناس	naas ناس	naas ناس	naas ناس	naas ناس
liseh لِسَه	liseh لِسَه	liseh لِسَه	liheseh ليهَسَه	liHed 'elaa'n لِحَد ألآن
mish مِش	mish مِش	mish/moo مِش/مو	moo مو	leyse لَيْسَ
mushkileh مُشْكِلَة	mushkileh مُشْكِلَة	mishkile مِشْكِلِ	mushkileh مُشْكِلَة	mushkileh مُشْكِلَة
'ekeed أكيد	'ekeed أكيد	'ekeed أكيد	'ekeed أكيد	'ekeed أكيد
mebrook مَبْروك	mebrook مَبْروك	mebrook مَبْروك	mebrook مَبْروك	mebrook مَبْروك
jiden جِداً	jiden/'ewee جِداً/أوي	jiden/kiteer جِداً/كتير	jiden/hwaayeh جِداً/هْوايَه	jiden جِداً
'oofees أوفيس	'oofees أوفيس	'oofees أوفيس	'oofees أوفيس	mekteb مَكْتَب
hiye هِيَ	hiyeh هِيَه	hiyeh هِيَه	hiyeh هِيَه	hiye هِيَ
lugheh لُغَة	lugheh لُغَة	lugheh لُغَة	lugheh لُغَة	lugheh لُغَة
dewleh دَوْلَة	dewleh دَوْلَة	dewleh دَوْلَة	dewleh دَوْلَة	dewleh دَوْلَة
muhim مُهِم	muhim مُهِم	mhim مهِم	muhim مُهِم	muhim مُهِم
muhimeh مُهِمَة	muhimeh مُهِمَة	mhimi مهِمِ	muhimeh مُهِمَة	muhimeh مُهِمَة
baalkoon بالكون	belakooneh بَلَكونَه	belakooneh بَلَكونَه	baalkoon بالكون	shurfeh شُرْفَة
fustaan فُسْتان	fustaan فُسْتان	fistaan فِسْتان	fistaan فِسْتان	fustaan فُسْتان
'inti إنْتِ	'inti إنْتِ	'inti إنْتِ	'inti إنْتِ	'inti إنْتِ
Sedeeqeh صَديقَة	Sedee'eh صَديءَة	Sedee'eh صَديءَة	Sedeeqeh صَديقَة	Sedeeqeh صَديقَة
'eSdiqaa' أصْدِقاء	ء for qaaf in Egypt	'eSdiqaa' أصْدِقاء	'eSdiqaa' أصْدِقاء	'eSdiqaa' أصْدِقاء
'eqaaribee أقاربي	'uraayibinee أرَيِّبيني	'uraayibinee أرَيِّبيني	'eqaaribee أقاربي	'eqaaribee أقاربي
fiAl فِعل	fiAl فِعل	fiAil فِعِل	fiAil فِعِل	fiAl فِعل
hum هُم	hum هُم	hine هِنَّ	humeh هُمَه	hum هُم
'intoo إنْتو	'intoo إنْتو	'intun إنْتُنْ	'intoo إنْتو	'entum أنْتُم
shee شي	shee شي	shee شي	shee شي	shey' شَيء
'elaan ألآن	dil we'tee دِلْ وَعْتِ	hellaa هَلّا	heseh/'ilHeen هَسَه	'elaan ألآن
raaH راح	He حَ	He حَ	raaH راح	sewfe سَوْفَ
raaH 'enaam راح أنام	Henaam حَنام	Henaam حَنام	raaH 'enaam راح أنام	sewfe 'enaam سَوْفَ أنام

Spoken Arabic for English Speakers

Chart of Learned Verbs in Four Major Arabic Dialects

Learned Verbs	Egyptian	Mediterranean	Gulf	FuSHaw
yenaam ينام	yinaam ينام	yenaam ينام	yenaam ينام	yenaam يَنام
yejeeb يجيب	yigeeb يجيب	yejeeb يجيب	yejeeb يجيب	yejlub يَجْلُب
yeshoof يشوف	yishoof يشوف	yeshoof يشوف	yeshoof يشوف	yeraw يَرى
yerooH يروح	yirooH يروح	yerooH يروح	yerooH يروح	yedhheb يَذهَب
yesewwee يسوّي	yiAmil يَعمِل	yesaawwee يساوي	yesewwee يسوّي	yeAmel يَعمَل
yimshee يمشي	yimshee يمشي	yimshee يمشي	yimshee يمشي	yemshee يَمشي
yeqool يقول	yi'ool يءول	yi'qool يءول	yegool يكول	yeqool يَقول
yeqoom يقوم	yi'oom يءوم	ye'oom يءوم	yegoom يكوم	yenheD يَنهَض
yiHkee يحكي	yiHkee يحكي	yiHkee يحكي	yichee يحجي	yeHkee يَحكي
yiHtaaj يحتاج	yiHtaag يحتاك	yiHtaaj يحتاج	yiHtaaj يحتاج	yeHtaaj يَحتاج
yilAeb يلعَب	yilAeb يلعَب	yilAeb يلعَب	yilAeb يلعَب	yelAeb يَلعَب
yereed يريد	Aaawiz عاوز	bidoo بدو	yereed يريد	yureed يُريد
yeHiss يحسّ	yiHiss يحسّ	yeHiss يحسّ	yeHiss يحسّ	yeHiss يَحسّ
yefekir يفكر	yifekir يفكر	yefekir يفكر	yefekir يفكر	yufekir يُفَكِر
yesteAmil يستَعمِل	yistiAmil يستعمل	yesteAmil يستعمل	yesteAmil يستعمل	yestekhdim يَستَخدِم
yiATie يعطي	yiATie يعطي	yiATee يعطي	yiATee يعطي	yeATee يَعطي
yeHib يحب	yiHib يحب	yeHib يحب	yeHib يحب	yuHib يُحِب
yezoor يزور	yizoor يزور	yezoor يزور	yezoor يزور	yezoor يَزور
yeneZZif ينَظِف	yinezzif ينَزِف	yeneddif ينَدِف	yeneZZif ينَظِف	yuneZZif يُنَظِف
yekoon يكون	yikoon يكون	yekoon يكون	yekoon يكون	yekoon يَكون
yimlik يملك	yimlik يملك	yimlik يملك	yimlik يملك	yemtelik يَمتَلِك
yesheel يشيل	yisheel يشيل	yesheel يشيل	yesheel يشيل	yesheel يَشيل
yeSeer يصير	yiSeer يصير	yeSeer يصير	yeSeer يصير	yeSeer يَصير
yeHuT يحط	yiHuT يحط	yeHuT يحط	yeHuT يحط	yeHuT يَحُط
yaakul ياكل	yaakul ياكل	yaakul ياكل	yaakul ياكل	yaa'kul يَأكُل
yaakhudh ياخذ	yaakhudh ياخذ	yaakhud ياخذ	yaakhudh ياخذ	yaa'khudh يَأخُذ
yitkellem يتكلّم	yitkellim يتكلّم	yitkellem يتكلّم	yitkellim يتكلّم	yetekellem يَتَكَلّم
yitAllem يتعلّم	yitAllim يتعلّم	yitAllem يتعلّم	yitAllem يتعلّم	yeteAllem يَتَعَلّم
yismeA يسمَع	yismeA يسمَع	yismeA يسمَع	yismeA يسمَع	yesmeA يَسمَع
yiktib يكتِب	yiktib يكتِب	yiktib يكتِب	yiktib يكتِب	yektub يَكتُب
yiTlub يطلُب	yiTlub يطلُب	yiTlub يطلُب	yiTlub يطلُب	yeTlub يَطلُب
yidrus يدرُس	yidris يدرِس	yidris يدرِس	yidrus يدرُس	yedrus يَدرُس
yiTbukh يطبُخ	yiTbukh يطبُخ	yiTbukh يطبُخ	yiTbukh يطبُخ	yeTbukh يَطبُخ
yiqreaa' يقرأ	yi'reaa يءرأ	yiqreaa يقرا	yiqreaa' يقرأ	yeqreaa' يَقرأ
yiAnee يعني	yiAnee يعني	yiAyee يعني	yiAnee يعني	yeAnee يَعني
yitfeseH يتفسَح	yitfeseH يتفسَح	yitfeseH يتفسَح	yitfeseH يتفسَح	yetfeseH يَتَفَسَح
yilbes يلبَس	yilbis يلبِس	yilboos يلبوس	yilbis يلبِس	yelbes يَلبَس
yitferej يتفَرَج	yitferej يتفَرَج	yitferej يتفَرَج	yitferej يتفَرَج	yeteferej يَتَفَرَج
yishreb يشرَب	yishreb يشرَب	yishreb يشرَب	yishreb يشرَب	yeshreb يَشرَب
yishtighul يشتغل	yishteghel يشتغَل	yishtighil يشتغِل	yishtighul يشتغل	yeshteghil يَشتَغِل
yinzil ينزِل	yinzil ينزِل	yinzil ينزِل	yinzil ينزِل	yenzil يَنزِل
yighsil يغسِل	yighsil يغسِل	yighsil يغسِل	yighsil يغسِل	yeghsil يَغسِل
yifAel يفعَل	yifAel يفعَل	yifAel يفعَل	yifAel يفعَل	yefAel يَفعَل